Open More Doors. Close More Sales.

201
Super
Sales Tips

FIELD-TESTED STRATEGIES
FOR PAINLESS PROSPECTING,
PERFECT PRESENTATIONS, AND
A QUICK CLOSE EVERY TIME

Compiled by
Gerhard
Gschwandtner

Founder and Publisher of *Selling Power*
and
The Editors of *Selling Power*

McGraw-Hill
New York   Chicago   San Francisco   Lisbon   London   Madrid   Mexico City
Milan   New Delhi   San Juan   Seoul   Singapore   Sydney   Toronto

Acknowledgments

From the many real-life sales stories published in *Selling Power* as Reader-to-Reader Tips, the editors have selected 201 of the very best for this book.

We wish to express our thanks to all the sales professionals who, over the years, have contributed their insights, expertise, and stories of selling experiences to *Selling Power*. They have given readers a rich and powerful history of the real world of selling.

Contents

What you will get from this book   4

How to use this book   6

The tips   8

Index of tip contributors   259

What you will get from this book

The selling tips in this book come directly from the field and straight from the heart. The *Selling Power* readers who have written them learned valuable lessons that shaped their selling careers. Such stories are all one of a kind. Shared with others, they form a core of real-world data that all sales professionals can use to expand their sales expertise. By trying these tips, or modifying them for individual sales calls, salespeople can stock a huge storehouse of creativity to draw from when the situation demands it. Reading stories and learning from peers can help you do better on your next sales call. With constant improvement comes more confidence and more successful selling. By reading the selling lessons in this book, you can practice continual improvement on a regular basis.

Stories are one of the oldest ways of relating information and transferring experience. This book follows a time-tested tradition of story-telling and story selling. The power in these pages can unlock more sales in your future. Read them for entertainment. Read them for pleasure. Read them for the lessons. Read them for information. Then sit down and write out your own selling tips. Share them with other salespeople. By teaching, we learn. By learning, we grow. By growing, everybody wins.

How to use this book

To get the most out of this book of real-life sales tips, think about the sales in your own career. What were the basic lessons you learned? When did you first start to feel confident? What sale taught you the most valuable lesson? Are you still growing as a professional? What areas need the most work? What plan do you have for self-improvement? Such questions and others should raise your level of awareness and spur you on to greater growth and better selling techniques.

To use these tips to sell with more confidence, study the basic elements of each one. Jot down what made the tip work and how you could use the same technique or skill to close your next sale or series of sales. Clip these notes to the pages of the tips that are particularly helpful to you and refer to them over the next weeks and months.

Keep this book with you. After a call that went well, jot down a few notes on what you think went right, what you could have done better, what you learned. Don't be judgmental. Simply record events and impressions. If a sale went badly, do the same thing. Try to analyze what went wrong then make a note of what you would do differently the next time you're in a similar situation.

Start to keep a log of your most memorable sales. Remember your past successes and failures and add to them your current sales experiences. Share them with other professionals and soon you will have a valuable asset in your own sales wisdom. Use these sales lessons to train new salespeople, to improve, by small increments, your own sales closing ratio and to reduce the stress that comes from repeating the same mistakes over and over. By following these guidelines, you can use these *Super Sales Tips* to help your sales grow.

I saw the sign

I sell signs—a high-visibility item, and almost every business needs one! Whenever I close a sale, I jot down the names of businesses adjacent to my new customer. Then later, after we've installed the sign, I send a postcard announcing the sign's arrival to those businesses on my list. Of course, I include information on how they, too, can get a great sign like my customer's. Response is terrific! Every time prospects pass our sign, they're reminded of my products, and the postcard tells them exactly where they can get them. This idea works well for those who sell any products used or displayed in the public eye: aluminum siding, painting services, paving work, brick- and stonework, roofing, lawn and landscaping services—the possibilities are endless.

Jane Connor, Salesperson/Owner

> **"Doing business without advertising is like winking at a girl in the dark. You know what you are doing, but nobody else does."**
>
> STEUART HENDERSON BRITT

Information, please

When you fulfill a request for product information, remind your prospects why they called or wrote for more information. If your prospects have too much on their minds to remember their request and what prompted them to make it, your literature may end up in the garbage with other unsolicited material. If a specific ad or product feature grabbed your prospect's attention, your response should take advantage of it. Instead of sending a deluge of information on your entire product line, customize literature packages with information on products or features in which the prospect took a special interest. A more personalized approach to information distribution may bring you more interested prospects and greater sales.

Ralph Pehrson, Sales Professional

Money well spent

As an advertising salesperson with the Gannett Rochester newspaper, I always closed my presentations to new prospects with, "I'll spend your money like it's my own." My words often helped reassure clients who were unfamiliar with costs, coverage, rates, and other factors that determine the price and benefits of advertising. In most cases, the prospect appreciated my concern and responded, "I think that's fair, and I'm going along with your suggestions."

Lester Edelman, Advertising—New Business

> **"Give them quality. That's the best kind of advertising."**
>
> **MILTON S. HERSHEY**

> "True luck consists not in holding the best of
> the cards at the table: Luckiest is he who
> knows just when to rise and go home."
>
> JOHN HAY

Cut the deck

I sell playing cards and I conduct a lot of business through trade
shows. Prior to a show, I will send a memo to contacts and clients indi-
cating what items are in the show and including five superjumbo playing cards. In the letter, I state that they should bring the cards to my
booth and we will "cut the deck." If any of their cards match the cut
deck, they will receive a prize. This has proven to be very successful so
far, and it entices more people to come over to my booth.

Amy Bruno, Area Manager

Parking lot presentation

Most salespeople can always use one more creative way to get an audience with their prospects. Here's mine: After hearing for the zillionth time that a prospect doesn't have the time to see me I respond, "Fine, then I'll meet you in your company parking lot. What time do you arrive at work?" The answer often throws my prospects off guard, so I explain that I've visited the prospect's office building several times and know that it takes at least three minutes to walk from the parking lot to the building elevators. I then say, "If I'm willing to meet you in the parking lot when you arrive at work, would you allow me to walk you to the building and talk to you for those three minutes?" One of my prospects asked me if I was serious, then offered me 15 minutes with him in his office the next day at the time I specified. When all else fails, this technique may get you that ever-elusive appointment.

Robert M. Peterson, Doctoral Student,
former Printing Salesperson

Organized gratitude

My salespeople send thank-you cards to more than 250 advertising clients who run ads in our weekly national trade publication. To simplify the process I drew up a simple log sheet for my salespeople that keeps track of their new clients. As they bring in new advertisers throughout the week, they take down such pertinent information as account numbers and contact names. Then, during downtime, they can look up each client in their computer database and send the thank-you note with a personal message and business card. The thank-you notes help increase repeat business and strengthen the client-salesperson relationship.

Carrie Anderson, Manager

Sometimes I say no

My company manufactures an application-dependent high-tech product used by petrochemical companies, manufacturing facilities, and municipalities to measure levels in process vessels. Specifying this type of product requires a thorough knowledge of the customer's expectations, the application specifics, and the correct product. In many cases our product is not the best solution to the customer's requirement, even though it may work. In cases like this I prefer to suggest the best alternative, even if it's not my product. This approach of saying "No, I think there is a better alternative than my product for this specific application" has built up trust and confidence with my customers. I may not make that sale, but that person spreads the word all over the plant and to friends in other industries. This source of referrals builds a strong and loyal customer base that keeps on expanding. This customer base is also more value-conscious and appreciative.

Don Nahrstedt, Vice President

Postcards from the show

At trade shows, where you meet lots of people and hold many meetings, try this great technique that has been successful for me. I get postcards from the city we are in and send the client/prospect a short note on the card saying, "Glad we saw each other, will follow up with the proposal, etc., next week." They see the postcard in their mail when they return from the trip, and it definitely makes you stand out from the crowd. It also reminds them of the meeting you had at the show.

Andrea Nierenberg, Sales Professional

"All letters, methinks, should be as free and easy as one's discourse, not studied as an oration, nor made up of hard words like a charm."

DOROTHY OSBORNE

Stamp of approval

Several years ago, as administrative assistant in the marketing department of a company that manufactures and sells equipment to radio stations, I was given the task of researching the Canadian market. We wanted to find out which stations would be replacing old equipment, when, and which products were favored. We also wanted to know what new technology was needed by the industry. I had to make sure we received good, reliable information. After pondering the best way to get the most returns, I hit upon the idea of using a Canadian postage stamp on the self-addressed return envelopes. I acquired the stamps through a very good customer in Canada and mailed a survey form to 295 Canadian radio stations, addressed to the attention of the station engineer. I expected a good return, but was astonished when 105 completed forms came back. It was evident the use of the Canadian postage stamp had accomplished a remarkable 35 percent return. During the following year, as a result of the information obtained from the survey, our sales team was able to increase equipment sales in Canada.

Nelda Hendon, Manager, Domestic Broadcast Sales

"Research is to see what everybody has seen, and to think what nobody else has thought."

ALBERT SZENT-GYORGYI

TIP #10

Faxed impressions

Here's an easy way to establish familiarity with prospects before your initial contact: Make a list of 10 potential customers. Next, use the decision maker's title to ask the receptionist for that person's first and last name and personal fax number. Tell the receptionist you understand that time is money and that you'd like to fax information about your product or service so that the decision maker can read about it and call if interested. Write a brief, warm, personal cover letter that tells the decision maker you'll be calling soon to follow up, and fax it to the decision maker with your product literature. In three to four days, call the decision maker, introduce yourself, and make sure the fax arrived safely. Your fax should help heat up an otherwise cold call.

Rita Peters, Sales Professional

Turn your prospect upside down

We can all use one more way to get an elusive prospect's attention. Use this technique to show your prospects that your approach is truly unique. Instead of sending the traditional business letter, type your letter upside down on your company letterhead. The idea may seem a little crazy, but it works. It gets the prospect's attention: Some simply want to know what kind of person types letters upside down; others feel that because your approach is unusual, you will be creative in problem solving.

Woody Galyean, District Sales Representative

> **"It's terrible to allow conventional habits to gain a hold on a whole household..."**
>
> **ZELDA FITZGERALD**

> **"America is becoming a nation of risk-takers, and the way we do business will never be the same."**
>
> **ALLAN KENNEDY**

Take a chance on me

Need an easy, inexpensive way to get a response from a hard-to-reach prospect? Send a lottery ticket with a short note that reads, "I'm giving you a chance with the lottery—how about giving me a chance?" That one little ticket not only gets my prospect's attention—it usually gets me an appointment.

Debbie Atchison, Sales Consultant

Survey your territory

As a new salesperson taking over a lot of dead accounts, I needed a way to introduce myself to my customers, find out more about them, and recapture their business. I found the solution in a survey. I mailed surveys to all my contacts, introducing myself and explaining that I wanted to play a larger role in their success. I asked questions that would allow me to recommend products to save them money. After a few months, I sent a second survey titled "Do you ever wish you could have things just the way you want them? Now you can!" The survey contained a variety of questions: Are you the contact person? What are the best times to reach you? Do I contact you too often/not often enough? Are you familiar with our complete product line? You might be surprised at the large number of responses you receive and how effectively the survey can build rapport and sales.

Cara Anderson, Sales Consultant

Humor by fax

The Dale Carnegie courses I've attended often emphasize the value of humor in the workplace. To keep my customers smiling, I keep a file of jokes to fax to them when the need arises. Amusing cover sheets, for example, help make my requests for credit applications a more pleasant experience. Over the years, many of my customers have returned the favor and faxed me humorous jokes and stories of their own, which builds rapport and keeps my own file growing. When your customers can count on getting a laugh out of your faxes, they'll look forward to hearing from you.

Laurie Jones, Account Executive

> "To know when one's self is interested, is the first condition of interesting other people."
>
> **WALTER PATER**

Shoestring selling

I always send out an introductory letter to warm up my cold calls, but I want my letters to stand out from every other salesperson's. In each one I enclose a shoestring and open my letter with, "Buying [type of product I sell] is about as exciting as buying shoelaces. Let me change all that for you." When I call to set up an appointment my prospects know exactly who I am, and my response is much better than the response to a regular old cold call.

Terri Job, Sales Consultant

Introducing...
your sales staff

As a sales manager for a temporary help company, I spend a lot of time on the road visiting prospects and customers. Customers often come in to place orders when I'm away from the office. When they do, they have to trust people they've never met to serve their needs, and I have to trust my staff to make a great first impression in my absence. Since I can't take my team around and introduce them to all my customers, I do the next best thing. Instead of distributing a fancy brochure describing my company I have one that highlights my team's experience and special talents. Customers love learning a little about the people they might speak with when they call or come in. One new customer even went to the same college and majored in the same field as one of my staff members, which helped create instant rapport. When your customers are comfortable with the entire sales staff, trust and rapport automatically increase.

Nancy Hahn, Sales and Marketing Manager

The "Friday Fax"

To remind field salespeople of current promotions, new product introductions, price changes, new personnel, or any other relevant information, my company sends a "Friday Fax" each week. At the end of every Thursday we fax a one-page notice to all our outside representatives that opens with a friendly greeting and closes with an inspiring quote. The "Friday Fax" is a creative, upbeat way to let your field salespeople know you haven't forgotten about them and to keep them informed in an appealing way.

Larry Easterlin, Vice President of Sales and Marketing

Bugging the customer

When my customers get really busy and stop responding to my faxes and phone calls, I use a little humor to get their attention. I stamp a Bugs Bunny figure on my usual letterhead and fax the page over to the customer. My clients almost invariably call back asking what happened to the rest of my fax, or they realize I want to know "What's up, Doc?" and call me explaining why they haven't been in touch. I always respond by telling them that when all else fails, I have to resort to "bugging" them for their own good!

Diana Mashini, Manager

Lifetime guarantee

To reassure our customers that their satisfaction is our top priority,

we offer them a written no-time-limit guarantee—and stand behind it.

The guarantee also shows customers that we know our work will stand

the test of time. We tell our customers, "If it's not right, we make it

right—now—no ifs, ands, or buts."

Jule Pels, Builder

"There's no great mystery to satisfying your customer. Build them a quality product and treat them with respect. It's that simple."

LEE IACOCCA

You word it well

My company deals almost exclusively with engineering personnel from large manufacturing firms. We try to distribute our technical data to as many of these engineers as possible, so we always ask our current contact for a list of other engineers to whom we can send our literature. At one time the question elicited little or no response—then we changed the way we ask. With our old method, current contacts didn't see how giving the names away would benefit their friends. Now we ask, "Is there anyone else there who might benefit from having our technical catalog on hand?" Because this question shows our interest in offering a benefit to our contact's associates, we now get a much better response when we ask for referrals.

Randy Cordes, Sales and Marketing Manager

Cash in on cover sheets

Gaining a competitive edge means taking advantage of every opportunity to raise interest in what my company does and what we sell. For an effective (and very inexpensive!) way to spread the word about new products or services, special sales, and events and other happenings, we use fax cover pages to advertise them. These cover pages grab the recipient's attention more than other businesses' cover pages and, best of all, every fax we send gives us a chance to set an appointment or make a sale.

Terry Grady, Director of Sales and Marketing

> **"If you want to succeed in the world, you must make your own opportunities."**
>
> **JOHN B. GOUGH**

TIP #22

After-hours prospecting pays off

During the early stages of my selling career, I often put myself in the

company owner's shoes and asked myself what I'd have to do to make

the company successful. For starters, I knew I needed to build my cus-

tomer base, but I was limiting my prospecting time to 9-to-5 business

hours. After a few months I began getting to work early, leaving late,

and coming in on Saturdays. I quickly discovered that my prospecting

efforts paid off even more during off-hours than during regular work-

ing hours. I reached the decision maker more often, and my success

helped me build a larger customer base and lay the foundation for a

successful sales career.

Stan Alie, Account Executive

Put your money where your mouth is

I came up with a unique and effective method to help me close a diffi-

cult deal with clients who insist my price is too high. I rip a $50 bill in

half and hand half of it to my clients, telling them that if they can find

a better value for his money, I'll give them the other half. Many of my

clients assume that I'd have to be pretty confident

to rip a $50 bill in half, so this strategy makes it

easier to get the order quickly instead of waiting for

prospects to look for a lower price.

Cheryl Amantea, Sales Professional

> **"What costs nothing is worth nothing."**
>
> **ANONYMOUS**

TIP #24

The salesperson's new clothes

My father is an old sales pro and the source of many creative selling

solutions. One of his best is a fun motivational idea we call "Clothes the

Sale." It started 12 years ago when we had an all-male sales team.

Today we have updated it to include all 60 salespeople, about 10 of

whom are women. Every year each salesperson in our company sub-

mits personal monthly sales goals for the coming year. Each month,

those who achieve their goals win an article of clothing that makes up

a suit—for example, first-time goal achievers always win top-quality

underwear; then for each monthly goal thereafter the winner gets

socks, shoes, shirt, pants, belt, tie, jacket, and so on. At the year-end

sales meeting and party, the entire sales crew must appear onstage in

however many (or few) clothes they won that year. Participation in the

program is completely voluntary. Instead of selecting the clothing, we

give the participants vouchers for top-quality clothing at the store of their choice. We find that we have 99 percent participation in the pro-

gram each year, because it turns into such a fun way for everyone to

compete on a level playing field for sales goals.

Jeff Colvin, Vice President

**"Clothes and manners do not make
the man; but, when he is made,
they greatly improve his appearance."**

HENRY WARD BEECHER

And thanks to all

I have taken the process of writing thank-you notes to all who purchase ads in our publication a step further than most by requiring our sales staff to send thank-yous at every stage of our sales process—to all prospects when they request information, to all prospects who become clients, and even to those prospects who decide not to take advantage of our services. This accomplishes two things. Psychologically, our salespeople are able to handle the rejection much better by ending with an upbeat thank-you for the time the prospect invested considering our fine service. Second, we leave the prospect with a top-notch professional impression. I have even had prospects change their mind, after initially saying no to our service, as the result of a brief thank-you note. This works especially well if the prospect was questioning our integrity, yet never voiced it as an objection.

Darron Richardson, Regional Director

A fair question

Salespeople often have to ask questions that make their prospects feel

like they're being interrogated, making them react by getting defensive

or clamming up. To soften the blow of a difficult question, precede it by

saying, "Is it a fair question to ask you...?" This technique helps keep

clients from feeling threatened or irritated, so they

feel more at ease opening up to you.

Christopher O. Jackson,
National Sales Manager

> **"Questions show
> the mind's range,
> and answers
> its subtlety."**
>
> **JOSEPH JOUBERT**

When you're smiling

When I was first hired as a sales representative at Clayton Homes, my

boss told me that the first thing I needed to do was find a way to

encourage my prospects and customers to respond to me individually.

I went down to the local bookstore and bought smiley-face stickers,

which I now use on my name tag, business cards, and all correspon-

> **"A smile is a light in the window of a face which shows that the heart is home."**
> UNKNOWN

dence. Now my prospects have a way to remember

my smiling face, and anything that helps them

remember me can't possibly hurt my sales. It's

something to smile about!

Renita Durall, Sales Representative

Upselling by design

As the owner of a desktop publishing firm, I find out my customers' budget so I can create an attractive design they can afford. Usually, they ask for an economical black-and-white design on colored paper. Once I find out what they want to spend, I create two designs: one in black and white that falls well within their price range, and one in full color that exceeds their budget by 35 percent. Many clients are so impressed with the color design that they choose it over the less costly black and white—and increase the size of their order! Show prospects you respect their budget needs by designing a proposal within their price range, but don't miss out on the chance to make a bigger sale by designing another proposal (and explaining its advantages) that exceeds their budget limit. Your customers might end up spending more than you—or they—thought they would!

Angela Batchelor, Creative Consultant/Owner

Chocolate triumph

As a television advertising salesperson, I've found that sports programming is very popular with my buyers. As each sports season approaches, I order chocolate basketballs, footballs, golf balls, or other sports-related items from my chocolate maker. I use the candy to put a smile on my prospects' faces before my presentation, and to thank them after they've bought. Best of all, you can adapt the idea to almost any industry. Team up with a small chocolatier who can offer customized service and has a variety of molds on hand. Almost everyone loves chocolate, and even if some of your prospects don't, the gesture may be enough to help you get the sale anyway.

> **"Any month whose name contains the letter a, e or u is the proper time for chocolate."**
>
> **SANDRA BOYNTON**

Donna Batdorff, Sales Professional

Ring-a-ding

I had been trying to reach the true decision maker at an ad agency for weeks. At first when I got his answering machine I just hung up. Then when I kept on getting his machine, I started leaving my name, phone number, and a brief message about why I was calling. This went on for about a month with absolutely no personal contact. I was very frustrated until I had a brainstorm. I started to leave a message with my name, phone number, and a brief message then, while I was still on the line, I stopped and started talking to myself out loud, saying, "Idiot, no wonder he hasn't called back. This person is really a machine and machines can't call back." Then I hung up. Five minutes later he called back saying he wasn't a machine. We both laughed a little and I got a face-to-face appointment.

Barry Katz, Sales Professional

The right touch

Research by Dr. J. Hornik at the University of Chicago showed that a light, brief (half-second) touch on the upper arm of shoppers caused them to shop 63 percent longer and spend 23 percent more than people who had not been touched. Dr. Hornik also found that timing was important. Touch someone shortly before you want that person to do something—agree to another appointment, buy something, whatever. Although touch has magic, it should not replace the handshake but be an added way to express warmth and a friendly desire to help.

John A. Quatrini, Sales Professional

What it's not

Many times when making cold calls to an executive at work, I encounter a secretary or assistant who wants to know who I am, what I want, and so on. The assistant does not mean to be difficult but is doing a good job of protecting the manager's time. I have found that the best way past this screening process starts with maintaining a firm attitude in your voice and then basically saying what the call is *not* about. For example, if I'm calling an attorney's office and am asked what the call is in reference to, I respond by saying that it is not about a pending case. Ninety percent of the time I get right through. I use the same type of process with other professionals and find it works almost all the time.

Marvin S. Goldman, Sales Professional

The blocker

This tip may seem simple, but when you have perfected it with the correct nuance, tone, and pitch, your success rate at getting through a prospect's screener can climb from 10 or 20 percent to a whopping 70 or 80 percent. Mine did! Here's how it works.

Screener: *ABC Systems, may I help you?*

Salesperson: *Good morning. Is Mr. Smith in?*

Screener: *I'll check. May I say who is calling?*

Salesperson: *Yes. This is Joe Sales. Who's this?*

Screener: *Oh, uh, Wendy.*

Salesperson: *Hello, Wendy, is he in?*

Screener: *Just a moment.*

This method establishes reciprocity with the receptionist at the first line of defense and, once established, it almost always works.

John T. Raisin, Sales Professional

Don't sell price

When I was asked to bid on a printing job for a local TV station, I made a proposal, and at a second meeting, the general manager told me they were still waiting for more bids. When I followed up by phone, the printed forms buyer told me my prices were lower than one company's but higher than the other. At two more meetings with the forms buyer and the station manager I was able to convince them to buy from me, although my prices were still 10 percent higher than the next-lowest bidder. How? I pointed out the benefits of buying from a regional supplier rather than an out-of-state supplier. I pointed out the experience and knowledge of our family-run business and all that implies in quality control and personalized service. I banked on the personal relationship I had developed with the station manager. I was persistent but patient over a period of five months. I sold quality, convenience, service, and peace of mind. I made a $30,000 sale because of my feature/benefit mindset.

Anup Gupta, Sales Professional

The gator letter

I hate it when prospects don't return my calls. Because I don't want to be a pain in the neck to prospects, I have developed what I call my "alligator letter." It begins: "Surely you must be so busy that the alligators have turned and eaten you alive." Then it goes on with a series of check-off squares and these lines:

- ☐ "I'm swamped. Call me after the first of _____ (month) so we can talk."

- ☐ "Don't call me. I'll call you."

- ☐ "Please take us off your list."

- ☐ "As soon as I get through this project, we can talk."

This letter goes out with a self-addressed, stamped envelope so all the prospect has to do is drop it in the mail to me. I have used this quite successfully and my prospects seem to enjoy it. Often they apologize for not returning my calls and explain that they just didn't have an answer for me at the time.

Roz Eaves, Sales Professional

Keep a goin'

Remember that persistence is not pressure. It is a release from pressure. It eliminates fear, inhibition, doubt, and excuses. It creates freedom, builds success, and opens doors to satisfaction. So, don't give up when a prospect says no. Continue to listen, question, learn, and close. Your customers will thank you for it and you'll be greasing the persistence wheel for many more circles of success.

Roy Bernius, Sales Professional

"I am not the smartest or the most talented person in the world, but I succeeded because I keep going and going and going."

SYLVESTER STALLONE

The customer comes first

A few years ago I was in the market for a new car. I knew what I

> **"The opportunity that God sends does not wake him up who is asleep."**
>
> **SENEGALESE PROVERB**

wanted and what I planned to pay. I decided to telephone a few dealerships to see what they would offer. Although I called several dealers, to my dismay the switchboard operator told me, "I'm sorry, all the salesmen are in a sales meeting." I was about to give up when I reached the last dealership on my list, where the switchboard operator said, "I'm sorry, all the salesmen are in a sales meeting, but if you'll hold, I'll call one out for you." Guess who got my business. Talk among yourselves at your next sales meeting. I've given you the topic.

Brad R. Lathrop, Sales Professional

Business is booming!

Our company actively works with its employees to help them understand that people like to do business with successful companies. To that end, when prospects or customers ask, "How's business?" we have been trained to respond with an upbeat and positive phrase. We say things like "It's terrific and we appreciate your business" or "We're getting bigger and better with every order." Remember, perception is nine-tenths of success, so if you want to be a winner, start sounding like one. And by the way, how's business?

John Knutson, Sales Professional

Get to know me

I have just learned the most important sales lesson—get to know your customers' problems. A local carpet dealer had committed to a regular ad schedule with my newspaper to coincide with a large display in our local mall. At the last minute he called and canceled the ads. Since I did not want to lose the business, I called and asked what the problem was. It turned out he needed a phone to do the mall display and the mall could not provide him with a hookup. I called one of my other accounts—a cellular phone company—arranged for a dealer demo for the duration of the show, and bingo, I was in business again. The carpet dealer bought the phone, the cellular dealer was happy, and I kept both accounts. But nothing would have worked out if I hadn't asked about my customer's problem.

Dawn Rowe, Sales Professional

A real smoker

I've seen a lot of salespeople burn out because of the high level of stress created by the way they handle rejection. Many of them seem to turn to smoking to let off steam after a rejection. I submit that there are better ways to handle the stress inherent in selling than filling your lungs with smoke. Along with your sales magazines and technical journals, subscribe to a magazine on outdoor activities or nature. If you can get outside and back into nature, whether it's a lakeside picnic at a city park or a hike up Mount Washington, you will find that concentrating on the beauty around you is the antithesis of the stress of selling, and you will immediately feel that stress drain out of your body and mind. I try to get out for a 10-mile hike at least once a month. Remember, it's much healthier to spend your money on hiking boots than cigarettes.

Allen Hefner, Systems Consultant

> "Father Time is not always a hard parent,
> and, though he tarries for none of his
> children, often lays his hand lightly on those
> who have used him well."
>
> CHARLES DICKENS

Please wait

Years ago, when I began my selling career, one customer used to keep

me cooling my heels in the lobby for 45 to 60 minutes before every call.

During the actual sales meeting, however, he was always congenial and

friendly. Although I would ask him if there was a better time to call on

him, he would just say that no time was better than any other. So I was

condemned to wait in the lobby before each call. After a year of this I

finally figured out a way to use this lobby time to my best advantage.

I'd sit down in the lobby, take out my paperwork, and begin on the cur-

rent day's work. I wrote call reports and follow-up letters, studied prod-

uct literature, and reviewed what I wanted to sell to this account.

Then during the second year of calling on this account, the wait became shorter, the customer and I began having lunch together, and, over the next three to four years, the customer and I really got to know each other. At this point he told me the reason why he made salespeople wait in the lobby. He said that most of them were not prepared for the call and asked him what they should sell him. His own sales force was highly trained and motivated, and he expected the same from salespeople who called on him. Today this account is in our top 10 and the customer has become a good friend who calls me to set appointments. My advice about customers who make you wait is this: Find a good use for your valuable time and don't waste it getting aggravated. Be ready to serve and you may just find real value in waiting in the lobby.

Daryl A. Allen, President

Read the want ads for leads

Many salespeople read newspapers as a source of leads by reading

announcements of promotions and news stories. I also find a good

source of leads in the help-wanted pages. For instance, many compa-

nies will explain in their ads the expansion plans or growth that have

prompted the new position. In addition, when I see an ad run by a

prospect or former customer for the job position I call on (i.e., human

resource director), I file that ad away for 60 days—

30 days for the company to fill the position, 30 days

for the new person to start in the job—and then I

call. Often I am the first person calling when that

individual is ready to make some buying decisions. I

> **"A good
> newspaper is a
> nation talking
> to itself."**
>
> **ARTHUR MILLER**
>
>

have penetrated many accounts by using this prospecting technique.

Dona Blunt, President

Set the agenda

Once you have an appointment with the buyer and you know the number of topics you need to discuss is extensive, fax an agenda thanking the buyer for granting the appointment and briefly detailing the various points you wish to discuss during your meeting. This agenda serves two purposes. First, it confirms your appointment and further cements it in the buyer's datebook. Second, it provides the buyer the opportunity to prepare for your call. Amazingly, it will often lead to the buyer allotting more time for your call simply because the agenda has been set.

Thomas J. Wilson, Key Accounts Manager

Still selling the sizzle

As a 21-year-old struggling with my first sales job vending wholesale paper and janitorial supplies, I wasn't having much success. I kept trodding from door to door, but the orders just weren't coming in.

Elmer Wheeler's book, *Sell the Sizzle and Not the Steak*, taught me to sell "sparkling" sanitary toilets instead of bowl cleaner, and "wet-looking" floors instead of floor wax. And wow—did the orders start rolling in! Find the magic phrase for your product or service and watch your sales take off.

Steve Webb, Sales Professional

> **"You can stroke people with words."**
>
> F. SCOTT FITZGERALD

Laid an egg lately?

When one of my best clients stopped returning my calls, I decided to appeal to his sense of humor! I contracted with a local agency to have a singing telegram delivered to the client's office by an actor costumed as a large yellow chicken. I personalized my message to the tune of "Happy Days Are Here Again" and left the rest up to the chicken! Early the next morning, a chagrined but laughing client called to say I had definitely captured his attention in a very creative manner! The chicken got me an appointment and restored our pleasant client/sales rep relationship. After several months, people are still talking about the day the chicken came to call. Never underestimate what a touch of humor can do for your sales!

Carol Gordon, Executive Director

Free advertising!

An effective voice-mail greeting can help you outshine your competition. Instead of using a run-of-the-mill greeting, I take the opportunity to sell my service. My current message says, "Hello, this is Paramount Cleaning Services, where we dry-clean your carpet with the HOST Dry Extraction Carpet Cleaning System. HOST is recommended or approved by more than 100 carpet and fiber manufacturers worldwide, and was top rated by *Consumer Reports* magazine. We're sorry we can't take your call in person, but would love the opportunity to serve you. So please leave your name, telephone number, and a brief message after the tone, and we'll return your call as soon as possible. Thank you." This message fits on a 30-second incoming greeting tape and doubles as a 30-second commercial. Many callers like to comparison shop by phone, but sharing interesting information via voice mail helps pique their interest and put your business at the top of their list.

Robert Ford, President

Mirror, mirror

I work for an online service and do 100 percent telephone sales. I have found that having a mirror in front of me and observing myself as I speak with customers by phone helps me sell. Without the mirror I often found myself doing other things and allowing my focus and concentration to stray from the sale and the customer, lowering my closing rate. With the mirror, I not only imagine myself in front of the prospect, but watch myself as if I actually were. This self-observation disciplines me to stay focused on my call and increases my confidence in myself, which in turn increases my sales.

Ginger Cole, Telemarketing Sales Representative

> **"Almost always it is the fear of being ourselves that brings us to the mirror."**
>
> **ANTONIO PORCHIA**

Hot cold call strategy

I sell a new product line to independent merchants. Invariably, the objections to carrying the product are the same—price, cash flow, shelf space, and timing—even though store owners indicate the product is clever and well made. When I make a sales call I have learned not to begin with the product and the value it adds. Instead, I first stroll through the store like a customer and assess the bandwidth of the product lines, high and low prices, and broadly estimate the annual revenue streams. Then I introduce myself to the owner, manager, or decision maker. I indicate that I am scouting for stores that would be appropriate to carry a new product line and that I don't want to take up their time if their marketing strategies and objectives are different from ours. This gets the clients talking and opens them up to probing questions. Frequently, I can tell that there are no clear strategies or objectives. I then summarize or formalize the key marketing strategy and objectives in a way that highlights the value of my product: "So what I understand is that you are primarily targeting such and such a customer and plan to move about X pieces per month year-round with a top price of Y and a Z percent markup. Is that in the ballpark?" This paves the way for a product presentation. Now I can personalize by referencing the store prices of other merchandise to illustrate the value of my product, how it fits into the present marketing mix, and how it will promote the sale of other items.

Joel Fullmer, Sales Professional

Start out strong

In our office, we have found a cold-calling technique that is not only consistent with our soft-sell approach, but also puts customers at ease immediately. As soon as our salespeople have given their introduction and formal greeting, they ask the customer, "Have I caught you at a good time?" This accomplishes one of two things: Customers are disarmed because they feel that the salesperson is empathetic and respectful of their time (making the customer more apt to listen and buy), or the salesperson can plan for follow-up at a later time so neither party's time is wasted. From the onset of the sales call, the key is to be proactive rather than reactive in your approach. The result is stronger rapport and fewer rejections.

Anne Richardson, Assistant Sales Manager

"All doors open to courtesy."

THOMAS FULLER

I just called to say "How are you?"

Developing a long-term relationship with an account requires more than just quality products and superior service. To encourage a lasting, profitable relationship I always strive to learn more about my customers on a strictly personal level. With this in mind, I have found it tremendously effective to ensure that at least every third phone call to each of my accounts is not business-related, but simply a call to see how the person—not the account—is doing. Encourage your customers to talk about their families, hobbies, and activities outside the office. Even the busiest buyer welcomes this brief social call, and we both enjoy discovering each other's outside interests. As a secondary benefit, a much greater percentage of my first phone calls are accepted, virtually eliminating unnecessary phone tag.

John Alofs, President/Owner

Pause and effect

I couldn't understand why one of my prospects wouldn't place an order with me—until I stopped talking long enough to let him make a decision. On my first call on this buyer, I extolled the virtues of my floor tile and its potential benefits to him while he listened attentively, but I left empty-handed and confused about where I was going wrong.

> **"One never repents of having spoken too little, but often of having spoken too much."**
>
> **PHILLIPE DE COMMYNES**

When I returned a month later I adopted a new approach, presented the basic product benefits, then kept quiet as the buyer and I stared at each other. This truly was a pregnant pause, because when the buyer finally spoke it was to place the largest order I had ever received. Apparently, my incessant talking on the first call had interfered with his ability to make a buying decision. Try giving your prospects a moment to think after you've made your presentation. A conversational pause isn't always negative—it could be pregnant with potential.

Thomas B. Porter, Sales Professional

The power of three

There is a simple rule I use when preparing sales presentations for my customers: Always limit the presentation to three reasons for buying the product or service. This helps focus the interview on the most critical ways I can be of service. The three reasons in each specific presentation will vary—much as customers' needs vary. I keep a list of 10 to 15 potential benefits that prospects might realize from my product or service. From that list, I pick the three reasons most likely to be relevant to my prospective client. The other handful of benefits is now ammunition for answering objections that may arise during the sales process. Using this approach will give clarity to your presentations and will virtually eliminate rambling sales presentations that are a waste of time for all parties involved.

Tom Trinko, Regional Manager

Don't do as someone else does

Many years ago, when I was an absolute beginner in the sales profession, I was employed for the summer by my brother, who was an outstanding salesman in the ladies' apparel industry. My job was to chauffeur him to his various accounts and carry his samples to the room where he would meet the buyer. On one sales call, he was really hot and writing a terrific order when he showed the buyer the last dress in his line. The buyer said, "That is the ugliest dress I have ever seen," whereupon my brother pulled the dress off its hanger, rolled it into a ball and tossed it over the edge of the buyer's desk and into the corner. The buyer looked in astonishment and asked Bill why he had done that. His response was, "I greatly respect your taste and if that is your opinion of that item, I shall seriously consider taking it out of my line." As we left the buyer, my brother told me to make haste back to our motel where he quickly steamed the wrinkles out of the dress. We continued to show that item to the rest of his accounts and prospects. When I actually entered the job market, my brother got me a job working for his company in a different territory. One night prior to an important sales call the next morning, I called Bill and asked him for some advice so I could start making some sales. He said, "Look, brother, you have traveled with me and have seen me sell, just imitate what I have done." The next day, as I was nervously showing my line of ladies' dresses, the buyer complained about the appearance of one of the items. I immediately balled up the dress and tossed it into the corner. Unfortunately for me there was a styrofoam cup of coffee in the path of the toss. It spilled all over the buyer's desk and I was promptly ushered out with no order. The moral is, don't try to completely imitate another's style, but pick and choose until you are comfortable with your own presentation and what works for you.

Lawrence A. Malin, National Sales Manager

It never hurts to ask

MarketSmart produces semi-custom promotional newsletters and post-cards for retail flower shops, greenhouses, and garden centers throughout the country. We respond to requests for literature by sending a comprehensive literature packet containing a cover letter, samples of our work, explanatory information on how the programs work, pricing and ordering information, and a copy of our newsletter. When I call prospects to make certain they've received the material, I jump right in with a nonthreatening icebreaker certain to engage them in dialogue: "So, did you like it? Hate it? What did you think?" When prospects realize that I'm more interested in hearing what they have to say than in making a sales pitch, they usually start talking. Even if they tell me that they're still months away from making a purchase, they always tell me what they really think. As a result, both of us benefit from a productive conversation, and I get important feedback from prospects on a daily basis.

Cathy Cain, Sales Professional

The price of quality

Sooner or later almost every salesperson will hear those five little words: "Your prices are too high!" One effective response convinces prospects to admit that high quality often costs a little more. When I hear the all-too-familiar price objection, I respond with, "Our prices are too high compared to what?" Asking that question in a serious, calm manner (without sounding or getting defensive) makes your prospects think about what they've said. If you sell to a business that prides itself on its quality products and prices its products accordingly, point that out. On a sales call to a fine restaurateur, compliment the buyer on a specific dish and say, "For the price you charge for that item, I am sure you use quality ingredients that warrant that price—right? What we offer (mention your product's attributes and how the prospect benefits) also warrants this price." This technique is applicable to most businesses and may change the way your prospects think about your product and price.

Lynn Potts, Sales Professional

A new use for the microwave

Humidity is high most of the year in Louisiana, and it's almost impossible to print multiple pages of the second side of a two-sided page in my laser printer due to the paper crinkling up. I tried to store our paper so that it would be protected from the humidity, but could find no dehumidifying cabinet to hold our reams of office paper. After enduring months of crinkled copy after crinkled copy, I tried microwaving the paper to reduce the excess moisture. I left the outside paper wrapper open to let the steam escape, and it worked. For the first time in months I could get 50 double-sided copies through my laser printer in a crinkle-free single pass. Even the print quality seems to have improved.

Mark McBride, Sales Professional

Elevator advertising

The next time you find yourself alone in an elevator, take advantage of free advertising. Take out a business card and print this message on the back: "Sue, please call this great sales rep and place an order! M." Be sure to sign with a first initial other than your own. Place the business card, note side up, on the floor under the elevator floor buttons. The card will stand out like a neon sign to any decision makers who get on after you.

James Mosvick, Sales Professional

> **"There is no such thing as bad publicity except your own obituary."**
>
> **BRENDAN BEHAN**

> "The best product must be sold. People won't come to you and take it away from you. You must go to them."
>
> **EDNA NEWMAN**

900 reasons to switch

I had been trying for three years to convince a heating and air-conditioning service to switch to my pager company. I knew I could provide better service at a lower cost than the service they had been using, but I couldn't seem to convince them to give me a try. I finally got their attention by writing a personal check to the company for $900, which is about how much they could save with my pager company in three years' time. Of course I printed VOID across the check, but my creative approach got my point across, and the next week one of the owners called me to switch companies. After three years, they're still with me.

John Schram, Sales Professional

A newsworthy practice

To (unobtrusively) keep my company in front of customers and prospects, I produce a company newsletter that educates my customers and prospects on issues that will improve their business performance. The one-page, general-interest newsletter familiarizes readers with my products and services. At the same time, it also helps build my reputation by positioning my company and staff as industry experts. Instead of spending hour after hour calling on prospective clients, I add new prospects to the newsletter mailing list. I've gotten terrific feedback from clients and prospects alike, who enjoy learning more about our industry and who appreciate my efforts to help them make better buying decisions by clearly explaining what I have to offer. When clients pass my newsletter around as lunchtime reading material, I'm confident in the knowledge that I'm providing a needed service.

Jennifer Triplett, Sales Professional

Research and (profit) development

The small training and consulting firm I work for needed to boost response to its direct mail campaign. We found the solution in going the extra mile for our customers. During information seminars, we often received dozens of questions but simply didn't have time to address all of them. Instead of leaving the questions unanswered, I took time after the seminars to research each question and send the person who asked it a personal letter along with articles and reference material supporting my answer. Over 50 percent of those who received the letters became long-term clients—about 10 times our usual success rate!

It took a lot of time and effort to conduct the research and write the responses, but the results were well worth it.

Rick Craig, Sales Professional

Follow up with flair

I use a personalized postcard for marketing and follow-up that leaves a lasting impression on my prospects. My postcards match my business card in style and appearance and feature my photo and slogan on the front. They're perfect for thank-you notes, short letters, or announcements and reminders of my services or upcoming events. In a business world that becomes less and less personal by the day, my postcard's personal touch helps keep my business relationships warm and friendly.

Joeann Fossland, President

I've got your number

When I got tired of time-consuming searches for phone numbers jotted down on scraps of paper, thumbing through database printouts for numbers, or calling information, I used my computer and printer to create a list of my accounts' main telephone numbers sized to fit a 3- by 5-inch space, cut it out and had it laminated at a local copy center. Now I've got a personal phone directory that gives me access to the numbers I call most in a fraction of the time it takes to flip through an address book or call 411. Both sides of the paper give me room for about 70 numbers for customers, airlines and car rental agencies (including club membership numbers), other members of my sales team, and general information numbers for my company that customers often ask for. The card also eliminates the need to carry more than a dozen hotel and airline membership cards and creates a great list of accounts and contacts I can mentally review for action items. I also created a credit-card-size version for my wallet with airline, hotel, family, and emergency numbers (e.g., my insurance company, doctor, and bank). For the cost of about $1, I have a convenient way to keep my important numbers at my fingertips.

John Kristoff, Sales Professional

"It is best to do things systematically, since we are only human, and disorder is our worst enemy."

HESIOD

Prospecting en route

I've found a great way to prospect smarter instead of harder. I always carry a clipboard in my car with a notepad and pen. Every time I drive to work or to an appointment I pick up a huge number of leads just by looking out the window. Here's what I recommend: The next time you're stopped at a traffic light, keep your eyes peeled for leads on the sides of delivery trucks, trailer sidewalls, billboards, building facades, lawns, or construction sites. Take notice of changes in your marketplace—a newly vacant parking lot or a once-empty lot now filled with cars. Get acquainted with mail carriers, next-day delivery people, and real estate agents who can keep you in the know about who's doing what that might be of professional interest to you. You might find yourself spending less time and effort prospecting, while increasing your prospects and profits.

Leonard G. Blumenschine III, Sales Representative

Thanks to the gatekeeper

When people ask me the secret of my eight-year sales success, I always answer, "Intense follow-up." Lots of salespeople send a follow-up thank-you note to their prospects, but I take the time to send a personal note to the often-overlooked receptionist or gatekeeper as well. The note comes as a pleasant surprise to many of them and sets me apart from my competitors. Best of all, it helps break down barriers, and on my next visit I usually get a warm welcome from the receptionist.

John Supplesa, Sales Representative

> **"Gratitude is the most exquisite form of courtesy."**
>
> **JACQUES MARITAIN**

Get your closing probability

The next time your prospect asks for time to think over a buying deci-

sion, say, "Mr. Prospect, that would be fine. I understand your desire to

think it over. But let me ask you this—when I call you back next week,

what is the probability, in percentage terms, that you and I will be

doing business?" This question requires prospects to give you an idea

of whether or not they'll buy. If they say it's unlikely that they will, you

can ask questions to find out why not and salvage the sale.

Rick Passaro, Sales Professional

Information worth saving

Occasionally, I will call on a client who is interested in my company's services, but does not have an immediate need. The prospect will usually say, "Send me something for my files for future reference." Rather than view this as the kiss of death or badger the prospects for more specific dates, which they usually don't know, I give them exactly what they ask for: our company's brochures and references—in a bright red hanging file folder. The view tab on the folder is clearly marked with my company's name and primary service area. This way, clients do not have to think about whether it is worth creating a file for my literature—I have already given them the information in a ready-to-use format. When I call back, I find that they still have my materials where they need them the most—at their fingertips!

Gretchen Sauerman, Sales Professional

Ask the experts

Twice a year, we hold training seminars for our 20 managers, who

cover seven states. For at least one of those seminars we invite sev-

eral industry representatives to sit on a guest panel of experts and

answer our sales managers' questions. For two to three hours, these

experts talk about what turns them off on sales calls, what new

products they'd like to see that our company doesn't provide, or any-

thing else our sales managers want to know more about. These

question-and-answer sessions have provided a wealth of valuable

"Learn as though you would never be able to master it, hold it as though you would be in fear of losing it."

CONFUCIUS

information and resulted in many new product

innovations and improvements.

Traci Esch, Marketing Associate

Telephone premium

Clyde Records had sold 348,000 people a record by comedian/musician Ray Stevens. With such a large customer base, they called on an Akron, Ohio, company for help in using the list in other ways. The expert's suggestion? "We developed a program that offered a set of two brand-new Ray Stevens videos, selling for $39.95. As an incentive, buyers were given a third Stevens video (a Ray Stevens TV pilot featuring various guest stars) as a premium. We told prospects they could keep the premium whether or not they bought the two-video set. We knew that some of these people would have already seen or bought the free video, so we suggested that they give it to a friend as a gift and keep the two-video set for themselves." With a response rate of 14 percent, much higher than expected through direct mail, Clyde Records converted a substantial number of one-time buyers into repeat customers.

Steve Pittendrigh, Sales Professional

Follow-up flag

I learned early in my sales career that follow-up is an essential part of the selling cycle. I was a sales representative, selling memberships for the Better Business Bureau of Houston, when I called on a fairly new oil change business. I went through my presentation and the customer told me that he would really like to be a member. First, however, he had to put a flagpole outside his business. He was a Vietnam vet and the flagpole was first on his list of things to do. I told him that I would contact him again when I saw his flagpole installed. I passed by his location weekly for a full eight months until, finally, I saw the flagpole go up. I immediately called him and reminded him of our agreement. The next day I picked up his membership application check. It may have been a long wait, but the follow-up call did pay off.

Debra Beasley, Sales Professional

Storm troops

Brainstorming is a great but often underused business tool. In a net-

working group I belong to, we frequently brainstorm

on such topics as marketing techniques, time man-

agement, and self-motivation. The group includes

salespeople, a CPA, a dental lab owner, a newspaper

publisher, a financial planner, and an astrologer.

They all have different ideas that others can adapt.

> **"An invasion of armies can be resisted, but not an idea whose time has come."**
>
> **VICTOR HUGO**

Sometimes an idea is new to a member; sometimes it's an old idea with

a new adaptation. I take the brainstorming idea one step further and

use it with clients. We brainstorm about marketing plans and where to

find and reach new markets. Drawing off of the ideas of others is a

great way to multiply your brainpower and your profits.

Christine Moses, Sales Professional

Business development time

When surgeons are in surgery, they are not returning phone calls, getting beeped, filling out paperwork, interviewing, or doing anything but operating. Similarly, I have found that salespeople need to treat their business development time as if it were their own version of sales surgery. I have developed something for my sales team called *business development days.* Once a week, we designate an entire day as business development day, during which one activity, and one activity alone, is undertaken: building new business. This means that there is no work on contracts, no meetings, no paperwork to fill out, no customer service issues to attend to, no anything other than calling for appointments and identifying and qualifying new business opportunities. In support of them, I pledge to protect the sales team from external intrusions into business development time. The day starts with a continental breakfast for everyone. At 9:00, everyone spends 30 seconds describing which list or which leads they intend to prospect for the day. At 9:15, the bell sounds and we're off to the races. We hold contests wherein everyone who contacts a certain number of prospects wins a prize (free lunch, a gift certificate, etc.). In another contest, everyone who confirms a certain number of appointments wins another prize. At the end of the day, we all get together to recap individual performances and award prizes. As important as it is for the salesperson to have uninterrupted time to conduct surgery (i.e., build the business), it is equally symbolic to declare that members of my sales team are indeed sales professionals and will religiously perform the most important piece of their respective responsibility: building new business. Business development days have filled both of these needs for me.

Robert N. West, Director of Sales

"To do two things at once is to do neither."

PUBLILIUS SYRUS

TIP #72

The referral
two-step

I have a little different perspective on getting referrals. It involves two

stages. The first stage—*trust*—involves building integrity, friendship,

and confidence between you and your customer. Before you can actu-

ally ask for a referral, you must become a trusted supplier to your cus-

tomer. The second level—*sharing*—involves asking the customer to

share his or her good fortune and good experience with you as a sup-

plier. Once you have passed the first level, the second should be almost

automatic. But don't be too proud to ask.

John Seib, Sales Professional

A little respect

To make my prospects respect an appointment we've made, I send out a letter confirming the appointment date. I enclose a couple of small, self-adhesive labels with my name and phone number and a place to write in the date and time of the appointment. I suggest that the prospects place the stickers on their planning calendar. As a result, I have far fewer missed appointments, and when prospects do break an appointment, they usually call me in advance and offer to reschedule.

Steven Donovan, Sales Representative

> **"Who breaks his faith no faith is held with him."**
>
> **SEIGNEUR DU BARTAS**

Prospect all day long

I keep a notebook handy in my car to jot down the names and addresses of businesses I pass that look like they could use my product. I vary my routes as often as possible and have asked my customer service representative to do the same thing. It's a great way to develop new prospect files all the time.

Debbie Shames, Sales Professional

"How many opportunities present themselves to a man without his noticing them?"

ARABIC PROVERB

That's why I'm calling

Over the years I have brought literally hundreds of customers on board by using one simple phrase. I use it on the initial call to set up an appointment. If the prospect says, "We already have a service," I say, "Well, that's why I'm calling." If the prospect says, "I'm happy with my current supplier," I say, "That's why I'm calling." If the prospect says, "We don't use a service. We do that ourselves," I say, "Yes, that's why I'm calling." This is a great way to set the prospect back for just a moment to give you time to speak your peace. I have seen many perplexed prospects who thought they had just shot me out of the saddle do a second take when I came back with "That is just why I am calling."

Gordon Hoover, Vice President

Thanks...for nothing

Send your customer a thank-you note for not getting the order. Why?

Many companies are required to get bids from different companies.

Sometimes these bids require many calls and lots of number crunch-

ing and, since you didn't get the business the first time, the buyer

may feel bad calling to ask you to spin your wheels again when a new

project arises. Your note will remove any strain and show you are a

professional who doesn't bear a grudge. Here's how your thank-you

note should go: "Thanks for letting us bid (make a presentation). I'm

sorry that we couldn't help you this time. Please keep us in mind for

future projects and feel free to call or fax me for jobs in the future."

Such a thank-you note leaves the door open for bids and sales oppor-

tunities in the future. I learned this technique many years ago from

Tom Hopkins—it works!

Alan H. Goldstein, Vice President

Eye contact

You can tell how your presentation is going simply by watching your prospect's eyes. If they dart around the room, check paperwork, or gaze out the window, it's time to shift gears. Say something unexpected or introduce a new idea, but do something different. Ask prospects what's on their mind and why you lost their attention. You might even want to cut the meeting short and offer to come back another time.

Dane Hooper, Sales Professional

> **"The eyes have one language everywhere."**
>
> **GEORGE HERBERT**

Good morning

When you absolutely have to get an appointment but a prospect won't

see you, try this. For four consecutive weeks, deliver a "good morning"

breakfast in attractive gift bags with sales literature and a note on cor-

porate stationery. Week 1: Bagels and a note that says, "Please enjoy

your breakfast with my compliments while you read my most current

sales literature. I'll be in touch." Week 2: Croissants and a small jar of

jam plus a note that says, "Please enjoy your breakfast and, when you

are in a jam, call on us." Week 3: Rolls and a note that says, "[Your com-

pany's name] keeps your business rolling." Week 4: Small loaf of bread

with a note that says, "[Your company name] will 'rise' to any occasion.

Call when you 'knead' us." During weeks 1, 2, and 3 simply leave the

breakfast with the receptionist or the prospect's assistant. On the last

week, ask to see the prospect to deliver the breakfast personally. Be

prepared to make a presentation.

Jennifer Jankowski, Account Representative

> ## "The reason why we have two ears and only one mouth is that we may listen the more and talk the less."
>
> ### ZENO OF CITIUM

Can we talk?

Over the years, I've learned that successful selling depends on your ability to listen. It's crucial to let your prospects talk about themselves and their business. Here is a good rule to follow: Talk 20 percent of the time, and spend the remaining 80 percent listening. My appointment-to-close ratio has increased dramatically since I made this change.

Justin A. Horn, Sales Professional

At least 10 ways

I provide prospects with at least 10 ways to use the product I sell. To compile my list, I call customers who currently use my product and ask how they use it. Once I have this master list, I tailor it to the needs of each new prospect. I learn all I can about the company I am calling on and cross-reference its needs with my list. For example, if health care clinicians are using a textbook as a reference in the clinic, I can sell the same textbook to professors by recommending they use it as a reference in the university library. As I compile my list, I learn from customers, and they feel flattered that I ask them to share their thoughts. This generates goodwill and future sales.

Diana M. Martin, Marketing

Listen up!

I sell advertising for a major national magazine. Like many salespeople I tend to talk more than I listen. But I'm working on it after one experience in my territory. I decided to call on the president of a small manufacturing company, hoping he would be able to set aside some time to discuss marketing his products via my publication. When he took the call I was surprised that he agreed to a meeting with no hesitation. In our first meeting he told me that he never gives anyone business until they have made at least 10 calls on him. Well, I made the 10 calls in a very short period of time and, when advertising budgets were allocated, we got the lion's share of this company's pot. Are you listening?

Denise Lovat, Sales Professional

Speak your customer's language

When I know my customers have been using my competitors' products and are used to their item numbers and product names, I know that this "language barrier" sometimes prevents me from getting the sale. Since my customers don't have the time or motivation to learn another manufacturer's nomenclature and item numbers, I make it easy for them. In the margin of my price list I added a column and use it to place our competitor's item numbers next to my company's equivalent products. This tactic helps my customers understand just what they're getting for their money and how my products compare (favorably) to what they already have. My customers have told me that this was the best thing I've done to earn more of their business!

Bill Cullen, Executive Marketing Representative

Call back later

Often a prospect will show interest in my product but will ask me to call back at a later time to go over details. Then when I call again, the prospect is often out of the office or busy. When this happens and I get the sense that this prospect is important and also very busy, I send an inexpensive gift—a small bouquet if the prospect is a female, a coffee cup arrangement if male—with a note saying: "I realize you are busy. I think my services would help alleviate some of your problems." This gesture usually elicits a thank-you call, and then I make the appointment.

Phillip D. Alcantar, Chief Marketing Officer

> **"You can accomplish by kindness what you cannot do by force."**
>
> **PUBLILIUS SYRUS**

May I quote you on that?

Your customers' praise is often the most effective advertising you can get. As I was returning to my lunch table during a break at one of my recent seminars, I overheard a participant exclaim, "Gary's tapes doubled our sales!" In response I immediately asked her, "Can I quote you on that?" She agreed, and I picked up a valuable new testimonial for my mailing piece. To get more testimonials from your happy customers, give some of your longtime clients a call and ask them what they think of your product or why they've remained so loyal to your company. Be prepared with open-ended questions to get close-lipped customers to tell you how they use your product, and use the information to help close future customers. Not only does "quote mining" supply you with valuable testimonials, it also helps reinforce your customers' decisions to buy and encourages them to continue to do so.

Dr. Gary Goodman, President

> **"Of cheerfulness, or good temper, the more it is spent, the more of it remains."**
>
> **RALPH WALDO EMERSON**

A cheerful good day

I am a sales manager for a small manufacturing company. For a short time, I also held the position of purchasing manager at the same time. In doing both jobs simultaneously, I discovered a little tip that I have passed down to my sales and customer service employees. When speaking with customers, always have a bright and cheery voice. Always use the customers' names and make sure they hang up with the feeling that you enjoyed speaking with them. This may be something everyone knows, but does everyone make an effort to give this to every phone call? We have found it very effective.

Lynne M. Taylor, Sales Manager

(Virtually) foolproof referrals

My favorite technique for getting referrals helps build rapport with the customers who give them to me. If my demonstration gets stalled or I'm waiting to talk to the decision maker, I always ask the support people, "Where did you work before you came here?" They usually worked in a similar industry doing a similar job, so their previous employer often has the same needs as my current prospect. When one person I asked told me where he'd worked before, I'd never heard of the company, but he said he thought they needed my product. He was right. The call I made to the company brought me my largest order yet. What better way to find out about qualified prospects?

Nancy Colligan, Sales Representative

An easier introduction

When making sales calls door-to-door, I always make sure I'm holding my computer and/or briefcase in my left hand, so my right is free to shake my prospect's hand. I can make a more professional impression if I'm not fumbling with whatever I'm carrying and can shake hands easily. Also, instead of facing the door, I stand sideways so my prospects can get a look at me before I see them and I don't look as though I'm peering into their homes ready to pounce on them. The more I can do to put my prospects at ease, the more likely they are to listen and perhaps buy.

Claude Peltz, CLU, ChFC

Don't be shy

When prospects call our company and don't leave a message, that leaves us no chance to earn their business. Now our voice-mail message tells them what's in it for them when they leave a message. Our automated greeting promises a $5.00 gift certificate to any caller who doesn't receive a callback within two hours. At first we thought $5.00 wouldn't convince people to leave a message when they didn't want to, but we've found that our callers often time us and are disappointed when we call before our time's up. Our voice-mail system tells us when the call was placed so we know when to start timing ourselves, and after responding to around 8,000 phone calls, we've had to give out only three gift certificates. When customers forget to leave their numbers, we just save the message until they call back and ask for their certificate. With this idea, we get a chance to turn all our callers into customers.

Kevin Swark, General Manager

Promise in writing

To show we're committed to great service, at the beginning of each year my account executives give their customers a list of the 10 services they personally guarantee to perform for them (e.g., returning phone calls on the same day). This lets customers know exactly what kind of service they can expect and invites them to complain when the salesperson doesn't meet those expectations.

Vincent Capozzi,
Director of Municipal Business

> **"To oblige persons often costs little and helps much."**
>
> **BALTASAR GRACIAN**

Pages of success

This motivational sales tool has lasting impact on my sales team and generates positive publicity for our company. We award salespeople a new book for their sales library for every testimonial letter they receive. With this reward, the salesperson wins with a valuable testimonial to show prospects how happy other customers are with our product. Plus, we circulate these testimonials throughout the company and present the books to the salespeople at a sales meeting, so they are recognized for a job well done. The company benefits by keeping a master book of testimonial letters to help when we solicit a national account. What's more, this program educates our salespeople (they're more eager to read books they've won) while it motivates them.

> **"Books give not wisdom where was none before, / But where some is, there reading makes it more."**
>
> **SIR JOHN HARINGTON**

Linda P. Kester, Sales Professional

> **"Flowers and plants are silent presences,
> they nourish every sense except the ear."**
>
> **MAY SARTON**

Sales in bloom

About five years ago, we came up with a sincere, warm (but not too personal) way to show our customers we appreciate them. Each spring we design a flyer that includes a poem and thank-you sentiment drawing parallels between the rebirth of nature and the renewing of friendship and success. We then add the flyer to a packet of hardy flower seeds. Everyone seems to appreciate the sentiment, and one client even gave us a bouquet grown from the seeds we gave her.

Mary Anne Hogue, President

Recruiting more sales

Customer understanding is critical to making the sale, but finding out about a prospect isn't always easy. In addition to the usual product literature and annual report, I've found that a company's college recruitment brochure often tells me a lot about it. Designed to sell students on a company, these brochures frequently feature names and photos of division heads, including new hires, and provide such information as challenges and mission statements of individual departments that you often can't find in other sources. To get a brochure, call the prospect company's personnel department as if you were a potential job applicant or parent job hunting for your son or daughter. The information you find might be your link to a sale.

> **"Knowledge is of two kinds. We know a subject ourselves, or we know where we can find information upon it."**
>
> SAMUEL JOHNSON

Anne Miller, Sales Professional

Multiple-choice objection

When I hear "I want to think it over," instead of drilling my prospects,

I put them at ease by saying, "You know, Ms. Prospect, when someone tells me they want to think about their decision, it usually means (1) they feel the price is too high or value is too low, (2) they don't believe in my company, my product, or me, (3) they're afraid of making a mistake, (4) they sense the product may be more troublesome than the problem, (5) they think the product will soon be obsolete, or (6) there's some other reason why they're not making a decision. Would you share which category you fall under?" This approach usually convinces my prospects to open up, so I can help them without interrogating them.

Carlos Llarena, Director of Recruitment

> **"The aim of argument, or of discussion, should not be victory, but progress."**
>
> **JOSEPH JOUBERT**

Free distribution

To promote a new product (in our case, a new book) and get our catalog out to qualified prospects, we wrote to a target group of existing

customers promising them a free copy of the book if they'd send us a

self-mailer postcard requesting at least five of our mail-order catalogs

to pass around to colleagues. Many of these customers ended up show-

ing the book and catalog to an average of 10 other people, so we got a

lot of good exposure and quickly sold many copies of the new book and

of backlist titles from the catalog. Of course, we also made quite a few

new customers in the process.

Carey Giudici, Sales Manager

> **"The excellence in a gift lies in its
> appropriateness rather than its value."**
>
> **CHARLES DUDLEY WARNER**

Paying for attention

I often know my prospects need my products, but getting an audience with them long enough to show them can be tough. When I encounter prospects who are unwilling to speak with me, I make them an offer they can't refuse. First I ask them what their time is worth. Then I ask them to meet with me and tell them that if at the end of the call they don't feel they've benefited, I'll reimburse them for their time. In return, I get a commitment from them to buy from me if I'm able to meet their needs, and to provide referrals if they know of anyone else who can use my product. This tactic requires a great deal of faith in one's product and one's ability to sell it, but it can help you get the few minutes you need to convince your prospect to buy.

Donald J. Engels Jr., CLU

> **"Our costliest expenditure is time."**
>
> **THEOPHRASTUS**

Sweet-talking salespeople

When my car rental agents acted more like they were taking a census than making a sale, I had to find out how to make them slow down and warm up when asking customers to upgrade or buy extras. To solve the problem, I told them to treat their customers as if they were a friend's elderly grandmother who'd come to visit. Instead of asking, "Are you coming in or staying outside?" now they say, "Would you like to come in and sit down and visit a while?" Instead of "Do you take the coverages?" they explain, "Our Loss Damage Waiver protects the car with no deductible in case it is wrecked, stolen, or damaged. It's a great plan that we highly recommend. Would you like to take it?" This kinder, gentler way of talking makes the prospect feel special and sweetens up our sales as well.

Don Pennington, Revenue Sales Manager

Sales by mail

My partner and I specialize in collectible dolls, so to boost sales we

decided to create a free newsletter for collectors. Each issue includes

current information on the dolls, special events, and

information on retired dolls. We run inexpensive ads

in our local newspaper classified section under

"Antiques and Collectibles," and we advertise in

other state newspapers. In each ad we offer the free

newsletter. To each new prospect who responds, we

> **"Advertising helps raise the standard of living by raising the standard of longing."**
>
> **UNKNOWN**

send the most recent edition of the newsletter plus a welcome letter,

three business cards to pass on to other collectors, and a "sign up a

friend" form. The newsletter helps position us as experts in the field,

and as response to our ads grows, so do our sales.

Traci Warrington, Partner

Cold-call thaw

To reduce cold-call jitters and increase my odds of getting an appointment, I fax my prospect a short, personalized letter introducing myself, my company, and my product, stating that I will call in a few days to follow up. A day or two later, I call in the early morning or late evening when I'm sure the prospect won't be in. I leave a message stating that I'm calling as promised to confirm that the prospect received my fax, then I briefly summarize the initial letter and say I'll call again. This message gets my name in front of the prospect a second time before the final step: another phone call placed when I hope to find him or her at work. By this time the prospect has seen my name at least once, so I'm no longer a stranger. I explain that I'm calling again to confirm that the prospect got my fax, and to see whether I can set up a time to meet. I'm more comfortable when I first speak to contacts knowing that I've already provided the general introductory information.

Lain Chroust Ehmann, Associate

> **"The lowest of jewelry thieves is the robber of that precious jewel of another's time."**
>
> ADLAI STEVENSON

An "eggsellent" idea

If you've got a one-minute egg timer, you've got a good way to get your prospect's attention and, possibly, an appointment. Mail the egg timer to your prospects with a note requesting one minute of their time.

Should you get an appointment, bring along another egg timer and set it for one minute to show that you're sincere and that you value your prospect's time. Chances are, your prospect won't stop you after 60 seconds and your fun, creative approach will help you make a sale.

Kristi Gacke, Regional Director of Sales

Special bulletin

To announce the coming of our salespeople to their customers' territories, I send out an amusing personal newswire to all of our customers. Simply titled "Debbie's Newswire," it includes funny clip art such as a picture of a TV with the caption "Turn us on!" or an image of the sun over the words "Hot Stuff." I also include amusing facts about each salesperson, and a "truth or dare" section in which the truth is new product info and the dare is a challenge for customers to call their salesperson to find out more. These newswires often prompt customer calls to our office, and the salespeople report a great response from on the road.

Debbie Kelley, Marketing Coordinator

> **"Total absence of humor renders life impossible."**
>
> COLETTE

Business breakfast

To save valuable working hours and cut down on expenses, I encourage my salespeople to conduct business over breakfast rather than lunch or dinner. The meal is just as pleasant, but costs a lot less and takes less time away from peak selling hours. It also ensures my salespeople have eaten the most important meal of the day, so they're energized and ready to be productive.

Paul Fedors, Director

> **"One cannot think well, love well, sleep well, if one has not dined well."**
>
> **VIRGINIA WOOLF**

Worth a thousand sales

When it's not enough to tell prospects what a terrific job you do, show them. I make my points with a three-ring binder full of 8- by 10-inch photos of some of my company's past projects. When we finish with a project, we arrange a follow-up call with the customer, at which time we take photos of the job to add to the book. This special attention makes our customers feel the job we did for them is truly outstanding, and helps us get the referrals that make up 15 percent of our business. Of course, the photos help to enhance and expand what is already a terrific sales tool.

Frank Karycinski, Sales Professional

Money talks

To make a lasting impression on prospects at a large business expo my

company (and our competitors) planned to attend, I wanted to offer a

memorable giveaway item. I wanted something more

original than mugs or key rings, but I had to stay

within my budget. My solution was as close as my

wallet. I found a supplier of oddly shaped, clear plas-

tic ziplock baggies and placed a dollar bill in each

> **"Ready money is Aladdin's lamp."**
>
> **GEORGE GORDON, LORD BYRON**

one. On the outside of each bag I affixed a label that read, "Our CPAs put

more money in your pocket." This item was such a hit that the local

press took pictures that gave my company extra exposure and I got

phone calls for weeks from people who loved my idea and had since

used it themselves.

Terri Sommella, Marketing Director

> **"Ours is the country where, in order to sell your product, you don't so much point out its merits as you first work like hell to sell yourself."**
>
> **LOUIS KRONENBERGER**

Welcome Wagon

With so many executives and companies moving to the growing city where I live, I appointed myself head of the welcoming committee. When I learn that my prospects are new to the state, I call the state tourist office and request that an information packet be mailed directly to their business. Then I follow up with a letter welcoming the prospect to the area. This friendly gesture helps get my prospects acquainted with their new surroundings and makes their relocation a little easier. Of course, it also helps me make a memorable first impression that gives me an edge on the competition.

Kristen Quintero, Training Consultant

Something for nothing

When you know your product's the best on the market, sometimes you can convince your prospects more easily by giving them a free sample. When we go to trade shows, we give away samples of our cleaning products instead of other promo items. No matter what your industry, beating your competition often means proving to your customers that your product is superior. At my company, the samples we distribute allow us to put our money where our mouth is and do just that.

Lisa Corona, Sales and Marketing

> **"Presents, believe me, seduce both men and gods."**
>
> OVID

Butter up your buyers

The products I sell are in no way related to popcorn, but this popular snack has earned me the nickname of "popcorn man" among my customers. When I want to show my appreciation to prospects, customers, or helpful receptionists, I say it with popcorn. The microwavable packets are inexpensive, easy to carry and distribute, and don't go stale. Best of all, this idea sets me apart from my competitors and lets my valued customers know that when they need me, I'm ready to *pop* in on a moment's notice!

Bob Hill, Director of Marketing

> **"That's something I've noticed about food: Whenever there's a crisis if you can get people to eating normally things get better."**
>
> **MADELEINE L'ENGLE**

> **"Why is it that you can sometimes feel the reality of people more keenly through a letter than face to face?"**
>
> ANNE MORROW LINDBERGH

Second-look letters

Businesspeople are so inundated with junk mail these days that we know we have to make our letters stand out to make sure they get opened. We use a regular postage stamp on our prospecting letters, and often enclose such small gifts as pens or memo pads with the company name and phone number. The outside of the envelope (which may be an unusual size and/or color) often features graphics with funny or timely messages. We can't get our message across unless the customer reads what's inside the envelope, so we try to make the outside as appealing as possible.

Angela Vosler, Investment Representative

Don't overlook the log

Whenever I call on a customer, I never fail to check the visitors' log that's usually found at the reception desk. One glance often tells me who my competitors are, who they're calling on, and when. When I sign in, I give away as little information as possible, using a department name instead of my name and substituting my company acronym for its full name.

Many of the prospects I get from the log are already qualified, and I recently received a large order from information I found there.

Scott Pitney, Sales Manager

"The competitor to be feared is one who never bothers about you at all, but goes on making his own business better all the time."

HENRY FORD, SR.

Open for business

Six years ago, my family founded a consulting firm focusing on records management and personnel services. To give our associates an inside look at our business, every year we hold an open house. Guests help themselves to international cuisine while they tour our offices, view demonstrations of current

> **"A guest never forgets the host who had treated him kindly."**
>
> HOMER

information management software, and pick up brochures and business cards. A guest book helps us keep track of attendees and attendance. These yearly get-togethers are terrific networking opportunities and are a fun and easy way to increase business while projecting a positive image to our customers.

Tina Merwin, Office Manager

The optimum 15

As a financial consultant for a large bank, I advise clients where to best place their CDs, annuities, mutual funds, and so on. Bank personnel refer many of their customers to me, and I then call them to schedule an appointment. I was recently given a new idea at a seminar, which has proven to be successful. In speaking with potential clients to set up an appointment, schedule the appointment at 15 minutes before or 15 minutes after the hour. I have found that people show up on time (and sometimes early) and I have very few no-shows.

Wendy Wallis, Sales Vice President

The doctor is in

The pharmaceutical company I represent allows me to be very creative in my efforts to attract more customers. Knowing that some of my impossible-to-see prospects (female physicians of dermatology) were prescribing a competitive product, I decided to stage a "Ladies' Dr. Derm Night"—an elegant, classy cocktail/dinner event. The event brought all my prospects together to exchange opinions and ideas, and I brought in a well-known speaker to talk about some new therapies for diseases (along with the benefits of my products). Out of the 31 female dermatologists in my territory, 26 attended, and every one of them asked me if I would organize another event in the future. In my business, a two- to three-point increase in market share for the year is the goal, but I was able to boost sales in my territory by two points in just two months. Now I get hugs from those dermatologists I was once unable to see!

Debbie Preston, Sales Professional

Moving toward a sale

It's getting harder and harder to stand out from all the other sales-people vying for your buyer's attention, so a little creativity often goes a long way toward helping differentiate you from everyone else. Once I've spoken with my prospects and piqued their inter-est in my products, I send them our package of infor-mation. Since it can be tough to reach them again by phone, I send a fax, and in the space for messages on the cover sheet, I print a graphic of a moving truck or an 18-wheeler and on the body of the truck I type, "It's your move." This idea often gives my buyer a laugh, and gives me many callbacks that I might not otherwise have gotten.

> **"It's all right to hesitate if you then go ahead."**
>
> **BERTOLT BRECHT**

Shelley Naser, Telecenter Manager

A matter of trust

Your customers won't know they can trust you until

you prove to them that you always live up to your com-

mitments and deliver what you promise. To make sure

I get off on the right foot with my customers, I often

intentionally withhold my business card after my initial call on them,

but promise to send the prospect a business card when I return to the

office. As soon as I get back to my office, I write up a quick thank-you

note, enclose the business card as promised and promptly mail it off to

my customer. When you do this, your customer will be reminded of the

commitment you made to mail it and will see that you kept your word.

You might still have a long way to go before you get the sale, but earn-

ing your buyer's trust is a great start.

John F. Kirchner, Manager of Sales and Customer Service

> **"To be trusted is a greater compliment than to be loved."**
>
> **GEORGE MACDONALD**

Sales à la carte

Whenever we're holding a sales meeting, expecting a client to come into the office, or planning some other sales function, I fax a copy of our local deli's lunch specials of the day along with an agenda for the meeting or event. When the salespeople and/or customers arrive, they're usually very grateful that I planned ahead for lunch, which helps me build rapport with them and promotes an atmosphere of motivating goodwill for that day's function—and I share the credit for the sales or improved productivity that result. Finding out what's for lunch can help build teamwork in a whole new way!

Patricia Pollak, Sales Professional

> **"There is nothing to which men, while they have food and drink, cannot reconcile themselves."**
>
> **GEORGE SANTAYANA**

Too much information

If you wouldn't consider giving the same canned presentation to all your prospects, be sure to customize the information you send them as well. Because prospects often just want to know what they'll have to pay and what they'll get out of your product, think twice before sending them long case studies, statistics, or other highly detailed info they don't want or need. Instead, save their time by providing several specific monthly payment options, then briefly recapping what they get in return: "For less than $1,000 a month we can provide your organization with a product that will protect you from losses that would more than triple this monthly expense if you didn't have this protection." This gives your prospects realistic, concrete figures to show them that your product is a wise investment.

Mike Reis, Senior Technical Assistant

Pushing the hot buttons

At trade shows we try to establish a personal and memorable connection with visitors by giving every prospect who stops at our booth a large, attractive button with ribbons emblazoned with our company logo or a product we're trying to promote. We tell the prospect that if they continue to wear the button around the trade show grounds they can win a prize if one of our company representatives spots them and takes their picture. After our employee takes a picture of each person he sees wearing a button, he has the prospect write his or her name and phone number on the back of the picture. At the end of the day, we put all the pictures in a box and draw winners. We end up with a lot of free advertising from show attendees wearing our buttons all day, and taking the pictures helps raise onlookers' interest in visiting our booth. Finally, our company benefits from a much more significant trade show presence that leaves a lasting positive impression on our prospects.

Steve McCain, Sales Professional

Would the real objection please come forward?

When customers say they want to "think over" their buying decision, it's often safe to assume that they have an objection they're not sharing. Asking "What do you want to think over?" can seem pushy and intimidating, which probably won't help you uncover the real problem. Instead, ask, "Is it a question of price?" Then quietly wait for a response. By guessing a specific objection, you'll

> **"Thinking is the most unhealthy thing in the world."**
>
> OSCAR WILDE

encourage prospects to correct you by stating their true concern. If your suggestion is correct, you probably found out what's really making your buyer hesitate. You might be surprised at how much this strategy improves your closing ratio.

Micky Huet, President

Earth-friendly attention getter

Despite all the effort you might put into writing them, many cover letters are never read by the people who receive them. To save time and paper and make my cover letters stand out, mine consist of only two or three powerful sentences neatly handwritten or typed on a quarter of a sheet of paper. I made a rubber stamp reading, "Please accept my personalized note, I like to recycle," and use it to stamp each of my letters in an upper corner. This method immediately resulted in more calls for me. I'm convinced that my letters are read more often because of it and that it helps my prospects remember me.

Kari Koivuniemi, Sales Professional

> **"Promise is most given when the least is said."**
>
> **GEORGE CHAPMAN**

TIP #119

Call me back— or else

You can reach prospects' voice mail, but you can't make them call back.

Of course, you can boost your chances of a return call with a message

that's anything but run-of-the-mill. If my prospect doesn't call me back

after several messages, I make a joke out of my deter-

mination to get through by saying, "Joe, you're not

ignoring me are you? You know you can run but you

cannot hide." Or I'll use a humorous threat: "I'm afraid

that I'm going to have to sing my next message to you

> **"Men will let you abuse them if only you will make them laugh."**
>
> **HENRY WARD BEECHER**

if I don't hear back from you, and believe me, it's not pretty." My funny

messages almost always elicit a return call, but if they don't, I make

good on my "threat." Only a few of my prospects have been immune to

my singing!

Lisa Schrader, Business Development Manager

Your big day

Whenever follow-up involves a historical date that is important to the client, I use a milestone software printout. Milestone software is mostly shareware (evaluation copies are available at many shareware distribution sites on the Web), but I use registered versions of "News of the Past," "On This Day" and "The Birthday Chronicle," plus the commercial version of "Birthday Newsletters" by Expert. Milestone software collates important events, birthdays of famous people, and popular songs of the day, together with an idea about the cost of living at the time of the client's anniversary or birthdate. My clients are overwhelmed by the attention to their special day. I even use milestone software now to break the ice with prospects who have their wedding anniversaries printed in the newspaper. Does it work? How many other insurance agents do you know who get messages of thanks in their voice mail or thank-you cards from grateful prospects for their marketing pieces? It beats cold calling.

Tony Brezovski, Insurance Agent

Casual day every day

I used to go out every day and beat the bushes for

new customers in my suit and tie, but as the current

trend in corporate America seems to be dressing

down, with casual Fridays on the rise, I decided to

jump on the bandwagon. Knowing how important it is

> **"Know, first, who you are, then adorn yourself accordingly."**
>
> **EPICTETUS**

to keep my name and my company's in front of my buyers, I went shop-

ping for casual clothing, then had my name and my company's taste-

fully embroidered on it. My customers don't have to worry about

remembering my name, so they can focus on my presentation more,

and the clothing promotes a more casual atmosphere that helps put my

buyers at ease. My sales are up; many of my fellow salespeople have fol-

lowed my lead; and now more of my customers know me by name.

Jeff Burr, National Sales Manager

Door-to-door, floor by floor

As an authorized sales agent for Britt Business Systems, which sells Xerox copiers and fax equipment, I'm required to make 100 cold calls each month. Hearing prospects say no to my face can be demotivating, and I needed a way to keep moving toward my cold-call quota so I can reach it on time. With this method I can make up to 30 cold calls in an hour and a half: I choose a building that's likely to be filled with qualified prospects, then start at the top floor and work my way down floor by floor, using the stairs so I don't waste time waiting for elevators. On each floor, I start at one end of the hall, then work my way back to the stairwell. By the time I'm finished, I've called on every office in the building. While most salespeople are working to reach the top, I'm working to reach the bottom!

Erika Vogel, Account Executive

> **"I will go anywhere provided it is forward."**
>
> DAVID LIVINGSTONE

Quizmaster

If you're a telemarketer you probably talk to voice mail 10 times more than you speak with a live person. I've found being creative when leaving messages on voice mail is very effective. For example, keep trivia questions next to the phone. Next time you reach a voice mail, start your message by asking a trivia question about a related industry and ask your prospect to call back for the answer to the trivia question and the answer to his or her business needs. The answer will be industry-specific. You'll be surprised with the response you get. Test a variety of techniques. See which ones potential customers respond to best.

Cathy Steiner, Advertising Sales Professional

"To question a wise man is the beginning of wisdom."

GERMAN PROVERB

Five basic principles to show that managers care

1. *Don't devalue a salesperson's worth.* In addressing an action or behavior that needs to change, always take the salesperson aside for a private talk. Dressing down a rep in front of other people hinders progress and is counterproductive to building a better relationship and stronger sales ability.

2. *Listen with understanding.* When a salesperson wants to discuss something, make yourself available both mentally and emotionally. Listen to understand all the issues involved, not just the ones you find relevant. This may be difficult, but it will be rewarding—for both of you.

3. *Talk to salespeople with compassion.* When you have something to say to a salesperson, be honest but respectful. By respecting your

salespeople, you build a team of people who can be open and honest with you and with their customers.

4. *Acknowledge positive efforts and good intentions.* Whenever a salesperson on your team invests time and energy into improving performance, acknowledge it in a positive way. In other words, recognize effort as well as solid sales performance.

5. *Help uncover the talent in every salesperson.* Look for ways to help your reps uncover their talents. Motivate them to reach higher. Set little goals in small steps that, in achieving these small goals, will give them a feeling of accomplishment and growth.

Alan Cervasio, Vice President,
Global Sales Strategy and Talent Management

> **"A thankful heart is the parent of all virtues."**
>
> **CICERO**

Trick or treat

My company had been trying to talk with a large manufacturing company that was already using another litigation support vendor. We were determined to get our foot in the door.

> **"A jest often decides matters of importance more effectually and happily than seriousness."**
>
> HORACE

At Halloween we sent packages of candy corn with stickers that read "The Trick to Successful Litigation" and "ADM Treats You to Professional Litigation Support Services" to seven top officials at the company. Inside was information about our products and services.

The packages caught a senior counsel's eye; I was able to make an appointment. Our treats did the trick and secured an all-important first meeting.

Laura Garcia, National Accounts Manager

> **"The soul may be a mere pretense,
> the mind makes very little sense.
> So let us value the appeal
> of that which we can taste and feel."**
>
> **PIET HEIN**

Speedy delivery

The next time you're on the phone and the prospect wants you to send

information, ask if he or she is at a computer. If so, ask the person to

bring up your company Web site. This is a lot better than sending a

brochure, because you can direct prospects to the pages you want them

to see. If you have a page that lists clients you've done business with,

make sure you send prospects to that page. No computer at your desk?

No problem! Just download the pages from the Web site and put them in

a binder. Turn the pages as you follow along with the customer. Also, in

face-to-face presentations, if you notice that prospects have a computer,

have them bring up your company site while you walk them through it.

Joe Catal, Sales Professional

Easy reference

Calling potential customers without preparing for the call will not get you where you want to go. My suggestion is to do a little research—even the tiniest bit helps—and print out a checklist of important information and points to make before you call. This way you have an easy reference and will sound more prepared when you get someone on the line. I made a blank checklist and printed a bunch of copies; now I just grab one when I need it. My list includes the following:

1. *Contact information.* Include company, name, title, location, and phone number.

2. *Focus.* What is the main reason you are calling them?

3. *Points to make.* Write your top three or four selling points you want to present to the customer. Why should this person work with you?

Then I have a section to fill in after I speak with the prospect, which includes the following:

4. *Recap of conversation.* What did you talk about? What are the

   issues that they need help addressing?

5. *Next steps.* What do you need to do now (e.g., send information)?

6. *Additional information.* Include the secretary's name, best time

   to call back, and so forth.

This list is a great tool for reference during and after your call. Even if

you don't get anyone on the line, this list helps you leave a detailed

phone message and will increase your chances of getting a callback!

Brooke Aram, Sales Professional

TIP #128

A treat in store

Dropping off breakfast (donuts, bagels, etc.) to a valued customer is a common way to say "Thank you for your business." While it is a nice gesture, virtually every vendor does this, and it fails to make you stand out from the crowd. I found a creative way to thank my customers and make a unique impression at the same time. During the hot summer months when the day tends to drag, I drop by my valued customers' with a styrofoam cooler filled with assorted ice cream bars. The cost of the cooler, ice, and treats is relatively low, and it provides my customers with a well-deserved break. More important, I am the vendor who stands out from the rest.

Patrick Collins, Sales Professional

> **"There is always a best way of doing everything, if it be to boil an egg."**
>
> **RALPH WALDO EMERSON**
>
>

Meetings ℞

Are your meetings rather sickly? Get a doctor. Dr. Seuss, to be precise.

Announce to the group that you have an excellent book unsurpassed in

the lesson of closing the deal. Then take *Green Eggs and Ham* by Dr.

Seuss out of your briefcase and begin the discussion.

Your meeting will follow the trials and tribulations of the extremely

persistent salesman Sam-I-am, who has problems: His client won't even

look at the product and doesn't like Sam at all—a hard sell at best.

Although repeatedly asked to leave, the salesman remains steadfast.

Would your salespeople do the same? Undaunted, Sam uses the "Try it you

may like it" close. Finally, the client agrees to try green eggs and ham—

anything to get rid of this Sam-I-am. And that's all it takes. The client is

completely sold. He even likes good old Sam-I-am. A successful sale.

The lively discussion and important lessons will ensure a sales

meeting that is both effective and memorable.

Anthony S. Cicatko Sr., Sales Professional

The ugly baby

Knocking the competition just doesn't work. Yet when telling a potential customer all the benefits of their products, many salespeople cannot resist highlighting the competition's weaknesses. So I remind our sales staff of the Ugly Baby story.

If you are walking in the park and see a woman with a baby carriage, your comments on what is in the carriage should be tactful. If the baby inside is ugly, the mother can tell you her baby is ugly, but you certainly cannot.

Calling attention to the poor quality of a product a potential customer has purchased is dangerous. Telling someone "You made a big mistake" is close to saying "... you dummy." Any negative comments made during a sales presentation could be remembered and confused with your product. If your customer wants to comment on the weaknesses of your competitor's product, keep from agreeing and stress the strong features of what you are trying to sell.

Somewhere during my sales career the Ugly Baby story was passed

on to me. Keeping positive has always helped me promote the product I

am trying to sell in the best possible way.

Jim Moorehead, Sales Manager

Patience rewarded

After reviewing bids for a telephone system from our company and competing vendors, a local insurance agency's corporate office decided to send the local office a used system. That was the start of a series of calls to my office from the insurance agency's office manager, who was having trouble finding a local company to install and support the used system.

I called around and found a company to work with them, answered many subsequent calls for help, and over time developed a good friendship with the agency. Later, when they convinced the corporate office to let them purchase a new system, guess whom they called?

Philip Kennedy, Account Executive

> **"Character is the salesperson's stock-in-trade. The product itself is secondary. Truthfulness, enthusiasm, and patience are great assets to every salesperson."**
>
> **GEORGE M. ADAMS**
>
>

Big rewards

One day a customer who didn't buy a great deal from us came in and purchased a water heater. I got to know him and was delighted to hear he liked to lift weights, which was also one of my hobbies. Soon we were working out together. My customer began to buy more from us each month because of the personal service he received from my staff and me. By the end of the second year, his monthly purchases were 16 times greater than when I first started. Later our "small" customer awarded our company a $256,000 contract for a commercial job. Never think small when it comes to your customers—you may be in for a big surprise.

Michael R. Obermeyer, Project Specialist

Never give up

Reaching key decision makers is the key to winning the battle. Twelve years ago, when Commodore was still selling computers, the company advertised with most of our competitors but not with us. It didn't understand our position in the market and ignored us.

The marketing manager was the key to unlocking the puzzle. My sales rep and I filmed a video to explain our story and to offer insights into our market. We focused on capturing the manager's attention and securing an appointment. We mailed the video in a special colorful package. The next day the manager, impressed with our efforts, called to arrange a meeting. We sold a two-page insert, and several ad pages followed during the next two years.

During the Battle of 1812, a fatally wounded Capt. James S. Lawrence exclaimed, "Don't give up the ship!" As his direct descendant, I follow his advice—especially when it comes to making sales.

George Halo, National Sales Manager

Leave 'em laughing

When I get a prospect who won't return calls, I resort to humor and leave this voice-mail message: "I have not heard back from you, so I am going to assume one of three things: First, perhaps you are not interested and you wish I would stop calling. Second, perhaps you really do need to speak with me, but you are trapped underneath a large object and cannot reach the phone. I hope not. [I say this with some humor.] Third, the timing is just off. In any case, please call and give me some guidance."

I used this message five times today and received three callbacks. One prospect who called me was in stitches: "How can I not respond to those funny lines?"

Michael Ubaldini, District Manager

> **"Good humor makes all things tolerable."**
>
> **HENRY WARD BEECHER**

Sounds like a plan

Making a sales call without a plan is like driving your car without a destination in mind: You might enjoy a pleasant ride, but do you know if you got anywhere? I use a miniplan that asks just two simple questions: In this sales call, (1) what am I going to do for the customer, and (2) what is the customer going to do for me?

> **"Plans get you into things but you got to work your way out."**
>
> **WILL ROGERS**

For each customer, make a list of answers to both questions. Despite its simplicity, the miniplan sets an objective for the call so you use your time wisely. It proves you are a person who adds value and ensures that the customer is actively involved in the exchange of value.

Sharon V. Parker, Branch Manager

Answers

What advice would I give new salespeople? Get educated. Gather as much information as possible on the products and services you sell. This will help you answer the many questions customers will have for you. Don't become frustrated if you find yourself having to research the answer to nearly every question at first. Every unknown answer is an opportunity for you to learn more. If you read up, you will soon find that you have the answers on the tip of your tongue.

Scott Reindl, Sales Professional

> **"The great pleasure of ignorance is the pleasure of asking questions."**
>
> **ROBERT LYND**

A year in the life

When I was a 23-year-old salesman in Texas, I had developed dozens of accounts in the automotive finance aftermarket. Between two dealer accounts that were approximately 30 miles apart was a Chevrolet car dealership. One day I stopped in but was told the owner did not see salespeople, and besides, he was busy. I said I didn't mind waiting. Finally, the dealer appeared and I explained what I did and asked him about any needs he might have. He showed me to the door, pointed to a sign overhead and said, "Son, if there is anything I need, I'll be getting it from the company listed right out front—General Motors."

I told him that I admired his loyalty. Then I asked him if General Motors would continue having his name next to theirs out front if he couldn't pay his bills. He replied that he had seen dozens of fast-talking city boys come and go, but he had no use for me or my products and services.

Despite my prospect's reluctance, I stopped at this dealership every week for 52 weeks. Each time I came, I brought a new idea that showed value-added benefits for the company. The answer was always the same: "No." On my fifty-second visit, I walked into the manager's office. "You again," he said. I announced that this was my one-year anniversary calling on him and that it was time to buy from me now. And finally he did. Over the years, up until I sold my business, that account was one of my highest producers.

Ron New, Vice President, Marketing

Take another look

Years ago, when I began my career, a couple booked our photography studio for their upcoming wedding. They arrived in an old car, wearing very casual clothes, to see their engagement photos. When I met them I simply assumed that they wouldn't buy much. We sat down, and I presented the prints in a nice folio before projecting the images onto a 30-by 40-inch screen in order to interest them in a wall portrait. Then I offered upgrades on the finish of their prints.

This was my first sale, and I felt awkward. The two were close to making a decision and wanted some time to think. I excused myself for a moment and walked into a back room. This gave me a chance to regain my composure. I finished the sale and the couple bought a wall-size portrait. Considering my inexperience, this sale was a huge success for me, and I was proud of it. The couple paid for the entire order and left happy.

Then it happened. From out in the parking lot I heard the grinding, slow-motion sound of a car that wouldn't start. The couple reentered the studio. "Our car is dead," they explained. I had an uneasy feeling in the pit of my stomach that they wanted a refund. Instead, they asked if they could use the phone, adding that they were "tired of that car" and couldn't wait to get the Lexus they had ordered. I thought they were joking. They weren't. They called the Lexus dealership, which soon delivered a loaner car for them.

My first sale was truly memorable because I learned firsthand the value of never prejudging customers.

Mark Weber, Marketing Consultant

Little things matter

To create loyal customers, little things go a long way. Recently, I visited one of our customers who had received a business-card holder with a clock on it from us. When he saw me, he mentioned how much he enjoyed my nice letters and "goodies" that I had sent to him—especially the clock business-card holder. "I really like it, but the clock has stopped and I need to get it fixed one of these days," he later admitted.

> **"Things seen are mightier than things heard."**
>
> **ALFRED, LORD TENNYSON**

I also have the same business-card holder, so I checked mine for the battery it uses. I purchased a similar battery, personally delivered it to my customer's office and replaced it for him. The clock started ticking and he was thrilled.

The battery cost less than $2. However, the value of my customer's remembering my small favor is priceless.

Joan Freitag, Sales Professional

Persistence times nine

Don't hesitate to take on those difficult accounts. The rewards are worth the effort. When I moved from newspaper to network television sales, I started prospecting the nonactive accounts on my list. One was a store selling high-end outdoor gear and clothing with a well-known brand name. Competition for this business is extremely tough, and for nine long years I contacted the prospect,

> **"Everything comes if a man will only wait."**
>
> **BENJAMIN DISRAELI**

sending updates and handwritten notes on our news progress. Finally, I secured a position in his marketing strategy—not only a single buy for a specific storewide sale, but a yearly budget. In my work, persistence pays, especially when combined with great patience.

Donna M. Newbry, Sales Professional

Dough *svidanya!*

Think selling is difficult? Just imagine your goods—lost—thousands of miles away, dealing with the KGB and having a guy named Big Vic on your sales team. When I was vice president of the OEM Division for Epson America Inc., we had the opportunity to start selling printers to the Soviet Union. Deals were conducted through middlemen—resellers, if you prefer. Our deal would commence on three conditions: A letter of credit must first be in place outside the Soviet Union, no barter (e.g., timber, vodka, platinum) allowed, and no payment in rubles.

After the letter of credit was in place, Epson shipped $3 million worth of printers into Vochtochny, near Vladivostok. Then Murphy's Law took over. The letter of credit turned out to be invalid; our buyer no longer wanted to deal with the Soviet middlemen; and the Soviet Union collapsed.

As the printer pallets rotted in Vochtochny, the Latvians offered themselves as middleman wannabes. I gave them a mostly powerless go-ahead to take control of the goods, since possession was 99 percent of the law during the Soviet Union's collapse. They enlisted the KGB and its guard dogs and moved the merchandise 6,000 miles by train across Siberia and the Ukraine, reportedly to Moscow and into a KGB warehouse.

To salvage the deal, I turned to Big Vic, an aptly named 6-foot 6-inch, 300-pound Lithuanian, who went to Moscow with a suitcase full of blue jeans and U.S. dollars to find the middlemen and our goods. Our printers turned up in Riga, Latvia.

Meanwhile, the Latvians said they wanted two things: reimbursement for their "costly storage expenses" and to develop a long-term importing relationship. I agreed, sort of. In Latvia, Big Vic found that the "costly storage" was an open-air brickyard covered with snow and guarded by a blind man and a dog.

Afterward, through a series of complicated maneuvers, we sold most of the printers before they disappeared. Financially we broke even—all things considered, a very successful outcome. And incidentally, Epson enjoys the largest market share of any printer company in Russia today.

Oh yes, in Russian, *do svidanya* means "until we meet again."

John R. (Jack) Confrey, Sales and Marketing Consultant

Sing out loud

If sales are flat, try listening to your own voice. If you've been in the same position for a year or two or ten, you have said your opening lines thousands of times and made hundreds of basically the same presentations. You can rattle the words off without thinking about them. Sometimes you might say them quickly. Sometimes you might drag out the words. Most of the time you deliver them in a monotone. If you don't consistently have enthusiasm in your voice, enthusiasm for your product, why should anyone else get excited about seeing you or buying from you?

The musical *Cats* had more than 7,000 performances on Broadway. The cast had to keep it fresh at every performance. You have to do the same. Remember when you first started and made those initial sales? You didn't have a tenth of the knowledge you have now. You made those sales because you had 10 times the enthusiasm. Listen to yourself when you make your next call. Are you flat? Boost yourself and you'll boost your sales as well. Recapture that rookie enthusiasm and you'll be back on top in no time.

Patrick Shemek, Account Executive

Highs and lows

Build a stronger team environment and you'll see better efforts. At the end of our weekly sales meetings, we go around the room and share our highest and lowest moments. Sometimes these are work-related accomplishments that might otherwise have gone unnoticed. Sometimes we share information about our personal lives, which gives us better insight into what we as people are about. The "highs" are usually followed by applause, while the "lows" receive sympathetic remarks and suggestions for facing similar situations in the future.

Melissa Azevedo, Assistant Director

Learn from success

To help employees learn how to be the best at creating loyal customers, I have created a journal of thrills and disappointments. In this book I document real cases of stories that I have heard from employees and customers. Any employee is free to use the journal to learn from others. It's a great way to learn, and it's enjoyable reading. We have expanded the hard-copy book to an electronic format as well, so our field personnel can access this journal for actual how-tos. It's becoming one of our prized possessions.

Joan A. Freitag, Director, Customer Loyalty Program

A closing poem

I'm a big fan of Zig Ziglar. I heard him recite a poem from an unknown source that he said he committed to memory when he first began selling. I was so impressed with the poem that I framed it and hung it in my office. Whenever clients express unfounded hesitation in the close, especially regarding money or budget, I simply ask them to read it out loud to me. It never fails . . . we all get a good laugh and that leads easily into further counseling, where the true objections come to the surface. Here is that poem.

The Bride, white of hair, is stooped over her cane,
Her footsteps uncertainly guiding.
While down the opposite aisle,
With a wan, toothless smile,
The Bridegroom, in wheelchair, comes riding.
Now who is this elderly couple thus wed?
Well you'll find when you've closely explored it,
That here is the rare
Most conservative pair
Who waited 'til they could afford it.

Ricky Fitzpatrick, Sales Professional

Closing the eavesdroppers

As a trainer by trade, I sometimes pick up new teaching ideas when I least expect it. I train automotive personnel how to present and sell vehicle-service agreements. I was training at a dealership when a service advisor came and said a customer was concerned about repairs—perhaps we should talk with her. Instead of having the customer come into the office, we grabbed our brochures and pricing and went to the waiting area. We didn't pay any attention to the other customers waiting; we simply followed our sales track. We began with introductions, asked several open-ended questions to determine her specific needs and concerns, and had a nice conversation. Next we showed this customer the coverages she might be able to use, and she chose the one that fit her ownership experience and budget. The surprise came when another customer who overheard our questions and presentation answered the questions in his own mind and also wanted coverage.

Another customer joined in, asking additional questions about his situation, and he purchased, too. Three sales with one presentation! We hadn't considered the audience available in the service department every day. Since we were away from the traditional sales atmosphere of the dealership, our presentation and discussions with the customer were more candid and conversational. I've now integrated these techniques into our sales process.

Kimberly Greenhut, API Director of Training

Smoke out hidden objectives

Early in my lodging sales career, I was working with a woman in the CEO's office of a major food producer on a recognition meeting. My contact, who had been in the CEO's office for many years, was responsible for bringing the CEO and plant managers together to celebrate another good sales year.

When she came to see my facility, she talked about how Don, the CEO, "and the boys" would do this or "Don and the boys" would do that during their visit to our city. It sounded great. I suggested some unique options to help create the fun-filled yet informal atmosphere she told me was so important to the success of the meeting. By the end of the tour I was very enthusiastic about the prospect of hosting this event.

My problem was, my buyer didn't seem as excited as I was. I knew I had missed something, so I asked her, "I think we can do a great job taking care of Don and the boys while they're here in town. While I think you'd agree with me, I know I have missed an important point in your decision process. What have we not touched on yet?"

To my surprise, she told me she wanted to continue to shop around because my facility did not have a hair salon. I thought, "Why would Don and the boys need a hair salon? They're all guys." Then it clicked . . . her personal agenda. They were not Don's boys; they were her boys. She had seen these plant managers begin their careers and move up the ladder until they were operating their own plants. This was her only chance to visit with them each year, and she wanted to look her very best.

Well, we did have a salon at our facility; I had skipped it because it hadn't seemed important. I took her up to the salon, where she met the staff and booked her appointment four months in advance. Then she walked back into my office and signed our agreement.

It turned out to be a great visit for Don, my customer, and her "boys," and we turned an almost-missed opportunity into a rewarding meeting. I'm glad I acted on my instinct that somehow the sale was not quite closed.

Mike Fahner, Vice President, Sales and Marketing

Keep your options open

You've presented your client with two or three options. The client is

now ready to buy and selects an option, but you think a different

option would be better for that customer. How do you suggest your

client reconsider without opening up the proverbial can of worms?

An effective way to handle this is to agree—and then have an inspi-

ration. You introduce the inspiration by using the word *or*.

> **"Do not reveal
> your thoughts to
> everyone, lest you
> drive away your
> good luck."**
>
> APOCRYPHA

The client tells you his selection and you say, "Great! [pause] Or [pause again] do you think option B might be better for you because . . ." This allows you to congratulate your client on making a great decision to buy from you. It allows you to impart new information (or information you've already presented and the client has forgotten) to help the client make a new decision. It shows you are looking out for your customer's best interests. It also avoids using the argumentative *but*.

Whether the client changes per your suggestion or stays with his or her first decision, you've done your job, kept a good rapport, and made the best possible sale.

Patrick Shemek, Sales Professional

Always talk to strangers

Though it often feels uncomfortable to speak to people we don't know, sometimes it pays off. Recently, while attending a trade show in Miami Beach, Florida, I stepped into a room full of telephone booths off the main lobby. As I walked in, three gentlemen were standing around, none of them using the phone. I felt a strange stare—was I interrupting something?

I didn't mean to eavesdrop, but I noticed they were speaking Spanish. I happen to speak fluent Spanish, because I am the export manager for my company and travel to Latin America regularly. I didn't pay much attention to what they were saying, as they were talking privately, in low voices.

I ignored them and started to make my phone call. They seemed somewhat annoyed and walked out of the room. Less than 10 seconds later, one of the phones near where they had been standing began to ring. I guessed they had been waiting to receive an overseas call. I answered the phone and said hello in Spanish. Was Mr. Juan José García there? I ran into the lobby looking for the three gentlemen, saw them immediately, and told them that there was a phone call. "Which of you is Mr. García?" I asked in Spanish, "It's for you." I don't know if he was shocked because I spoke Spanish, because I ran out to find him, or because it was such an important call, but he was pleased and grateful.

He finished his call quickly and thanked me for coming after him. We traded names and business cards, and I noticed that Juan José owned photo laboratories in Costa Rica. That rang another bell, in addition to the telephone. Juan José was a prospect that I had been trying to contact for about a year but was never able to pin down! He is a huge purchaser of photo albums. I introduced myself again and briefly discussed our line of photo albums and scrapbooks. He was quite impressed. I just received my second order from him today, and the potential for long-term business looks good . . . all because I went out of my way to help another person.

Harold Goodman, Export Manager

A thing of the past

Not only is perseverance important in selling, but it's also important not to prejudge what the customer needs.

My most memorable sale came when I least expected it. I had been selling golf equipment for 10 years and had one especially tough customer. One day I pulled up to his store, and there he was standing in the parking lot. The procedure had been the same year after year: Make an appointment at his convenience, say a few nice things, and have him order the same product (as long as it sold out completely the year before). He would usually tell me what he would order when I made the appointment.

As I sat in the parking lot, it occurred to me that I was not reaching my goal of introducing one new product during the sales call with this customer. I knew our company made the best golf bag in the industry, and he had not sold one in the past five years. I grabbed my sample and headed for the door, convinced that going ahead and confidently introducing this product to my customer was the right thing to do.

After a few minutes of conversation, he asked me to replicate last year's order and leave a copy of the invoice. I politely thanked him and asked if he could spare 60 seconds to see the number one golf bag on the market. I briefly explained the features and thanked him for listening. He said he had ordered his bags from another vendor for the past 10 years, but maybe it "was time for a change." He gave me a sizable order, and we proceeded to supply his top-selling golf bag for the next five years.

As I returned to the car that day, I reflected that not only is perseverance important in selling, but I also needed to stop prejudging what my customers need, no matter how far back we go.

Peter Hiskey, Sales Professional

TIP #151

Oaks from little acorns

Back in the days when carrier-route code discounts were brand-new, I was selling these services for a well-known computer-service bureau that wanted big jobs. So did I, of course. However, one day I landed a small project with a Bell Operating Company (yup, this was before the breakup of AT&T). It was for only 5,000 records, and we charged some ridiculous minimum, maybe $50. Since the BOC was mailing to everybody in the small area being targeted, it qualified just about 100 percent of the names and saved some money. My company did the job, but not happily. More small projects came in for more BOCs, and more, and more. And the complaints from my production folks also began to come in. Why was I wasting my company's resources on these piddling jobs? The only answer I could give at the time, and which made a lot of sense to me, was "But, it's AT&T!" The point, I felt, was that the potential was magnificent. Two years later, as a direct result of the service relationship we had built, we were privileged to handle the two largest mailings ever done in the United States. The first went to every household in the country, announcing and explaining the effects of divestiture; the second went to every company, and even to every person in each company who had a telephone line, offering an AT&T company calling card. In fact, the revenue from those two mailings alone exceeded the total sales of all the other salespeople in the organization for all our services. The moral? Never judge a book by its cover ... or a customer's worth by the look of a single project.

Tony Ambrose, President

Valuable questions

Here's a great technique that takes little preparation time but can pay off big. You can work on it on your way to visit the customer or before you pick up the receiver to phone. It's called the "sales activity focus."

For each sales activity you take on during the day, ask yourself three questions. The first is, "Why am I doing this?" If you can't answer that one, you might want to reconsider undertaking the activity at all. Think of it this way: If you don't have a customer-focused reason for being there, what are you and they going to take away from the meeting?

Next question: "What results do I want?" Remember, the results should be measurable or should have a deliverable attached to them. If you focus on achieving results on your call, your customer will as well. It's the focus on results that moves you from being a problem solver to becoming an opportunity realizer.

But just focusing on the results is not enough, so we come to the third question: "How will I achieve those results?" If you've developed a brief plan or even just an idea prior to the call, then you are really using your time to the best advantage. You'll be seen as the one who has thought it out and is there to make it happen.

Marc Daniels, Sales Professional

Keep a journal of ideas

In our organization, we keep a journal filled with tips on how to go the extra mile for customers or fellow employees. One person maintains the journal and fills it with entries submitted by everyone in the company. Those who have difficulty coming up with their own unique ideas for satisfying customers can refer to the journal and see what has worked and what has not worked for their colleagues. Those faced with the challenge of dealing with unhappy customers can even look to the journal for encouraging tips on how to smooth ruffled feathers. The journal has helped us find ways to support each other and keep our customers happy and loyal.

Joan A. Freitag, General Services Administration

> **"Information's pretty thin stuff, unless mixed with experience."**
>
> **CLARENCE DAY**

Think big

Successful people believe in themselves. They visualize themselves as being successful, and they never let failure or adversity stop them. If you can see yourself accomplishing something, you can accomplish it! Your actions, thoughts, and even the way others perceive you is determined in large part by how you perceive yourself in your subconscious mind. So before every sale, visualize yourself . . .

1. Hitting it off with the person that you are meeting

2. Coming across as being knowledgeable and informative

3. Getting the sale!

Remember, you will rarely ever exceed your own expectations of yourself, so it is important that you visualize yourself achieving success.

Grant Blair, Sales Professional

Ahead of the game

As a former officer in the military, I was taught to arrive at least 15 minutes before any meeting to read the tactical map and get a general sense of the military situation. In my new civilian marketing life, I have applied that rule as well. Prior to meeting any company executive, I always show up early and converse a little with the secretary or executive assistant to get a feel for what big issues may be facing the company. I also pick up some of the most recent company brochures.

> **"Better three hours too soon than a minute too late."**
>
> **SHAKESPEARE**

As I set up for my computer presentation, I engage in some small talk with the executives about the big issues they are dealing with. I find that they remark positively on my ability to stay so informed about the issues facing their company.

By getting there a little early, I am able to start on the right foot and close the deal much sooner.

Bruce Poulin, Sales Professional

Be a standout

As a salesperson, you need to distinguish yourself from your competitors.

A couple of years ago I started attaching motivational quotes to my e-mails, letters, and correspondence to my prospects, friends, and clients. Every week I would search for new quotes, and every chance I had I would send an e-mail to all of my prospects introducing new products or specials, or just to keep in touch, and I would always attach one of the motivational quotes. When I made follow-up phone calls, some of these prospects with whom I had never spoken before would ask, "Are you the guy who sends the motivational quotes?" Or they would say, "I really liked your quote this week." Sometimes I would receive e-mails from my prospects asking me for the weekly quote. I was able to use this simple tool to get my foot in the door, and as a result, my sales volume increased.

Eder Holguin, Sales Professional

Customization pays

One shot at the business every seven years is all you get in medical capital-equipment sales. One afternoon I overheard a competitor bragging about a big sale he was about to make to an account my sales representative had not yet called on because he was brand-new. So we promptly headed to the account. As we sat down with the decision maker, it was clear that time was short and the decision had just about been made. We quickly reviewed the acquisition criteria and found that our product fitted the customer's needs perfectly. After some discussion, the buyer informed us that the vendor with the lowest price would win the bid, and he immediately asked for a quote. I refused! Both the sales rep and the customer were speechless. I told the decision maker that if price was truly his only criteria we did not stand a chance, as our products cost substantially more to purchase. I told him that before I could submit a price I needed to work with him to better understand what the real needs and issues were. Only then would I submit a quotation. This approach would ensure that he would purchase only what he needed rather than what the lowest bid provided him. Although he didn't like it, he went along and let us spend an entire day talking to the staff to determine their issues and demonstrate our instruments. By the end of the day, every staff member was on our side.

Two days later we submitted a proposal for our customized solution. We were one of three vendors who submitted bids. After the proposals were reviewed, I was rewarded the purchase order. The sale was worth $191,000 in capital and $200,000 per year in disposables. I later learned that the competitor who was boasting about the sale had submitted a proposal for $110,000. By not giving in and by developing a true understanding of the customer's needs, I won the battle over price!

Bob Gilot, Manager, Sales Training and Development

My top 10 list

I am the U.S. sales manager for a manufacturer of technical instruments. The following is something I pound into my sales force.

**THE TOP 10 REASONS TO ALWAYS
CONFIRM PRICING WITH A PROPOSAL**

1. *It avoids misunderstandings and mistakes.* Part numbers, pricing, delivery, terms, and conditions are clearly written down.

2. *It's a reference.* You, your correspondent, and your customer can refer to it when calling in an order or for general questions.

3. *It's a record.* A written quote is a document that can be recorded, tracked, and reviewed for accuracy.

4. *It's a trend indicator.* A record of confirming quotes and status gives an indication of territory and product activity.

5. *It helps with forecasting.* A list of quotations and status gives an easy, quick reference for major 30-, 60-, or more than 90-day booking potential.

6. *It facilitates follow-up.* Written quotes are easier to follow up on. They are put on a quote log with contact, phone number, status, and description for an easy one-page monthly follow-up sheet.

7. *Written quotes get filed.* Verbal quotes don't. Many projects are delayed or canceled, or users change. A written quote may follow the project, and when it's reactivated, you get the call.

8. *Written quotes travel.* Verbal quotes don't. A confirming quote may be kicked up or down an organization or to multiple users.

9. *It's a sales tool.* A well-written descriptive quote will help sell your offering by tying features into the description. Use a cover letter to further expand your proposal.

10. *It's professional.* An error-free, well-written quote shows that you and your company are professional.

Steven C. Tiso, Sales Manager

Never assume

When you meet new people, you need to let them know what you do.

When you meet new people at parties, networking functions, or even in the course of daily business activities, you cannot assume they know what you do or how it might apply to them.

When someone asks me, "What do you do?" and I reply, "I'm in promotional advertising," their response is usually something like, "Uh-huh," or "Oh, that's nice." But they don't really know what that means or how it can help them. So I always take time to elaborate. I say something like, "I work in promotional advertising. My company supplies custom-imprinted products like T-shirts, pens, cups, and key chains to businesses, schools, organizations, and political campaigns. We also offer graphic-design services." Then I might give an example of a recent client or a big project we are currently working on. This helps others conceptualize the possibilities of using our products for their own firms.

When you've just met someone at a casual gathering, you certainly won't be giving a formal sales presentation. But if you don't clearly communicate what it is you do, you will have missed the opportunity to begin a new business relationship.

Kelly Warshofsky, Sales Professional

Take my receptionist . . . please

As executive vice president of Lloyd Staffing, I am responsible for temporary staffing operations nationwide. In 1996, we were attempting to build up business for our relatively new Manhattan location. In particular, I had been trying to get business from a major company with offices throughout the tristate area.

My contact at this company finally gave us an order for a temporary receptionist, but he gave us less than one full day to find a candidate. I knew it was critical to make a good impression, and I wanted to send the most qualified candidate. At the time, our receptionist was on vacation, and we had a temporary receptionist filling in who was seeking a full-time, permanent position. I decided to send her to fill the order. She was highly qualified, and I knew she could handle the job.

Initially, my client didn't realize that this was the receptionist from our office, but he was thrilled with her capabilities. In fact, he was so happy with her performance that he hired her for a full-time position. He then learned that she had been a Lloyd employee and realized what we had done to fill the order. He was so impressed with the quality of our service that from this point on he provided us with additional business. When our contact moved to another company, he continued to use Lloyd, and this new company became another key account for us. I am happy to say that six years have passed and we still maintain a solid relationship with the client and our contact. This contact has also served as a great reference.

In our industry, service is key, so I made a decision that demonstrated our willingness to go above and beyond what is expected to develop a long-lasting, quality relationship with clients. It certainly paid off.

Keith Banks, Executive Vice President

After the fact

If you want repeat business, then use the after-action review (AAR) strategy.

Every time we finish one of our sales or customer-service sessions, we have participants complete evaluations before they leave. Management and employees participate. We then conduct a statistical analysis of the information, including participant comments. Within 10 days a report is sent to the contact person and to company executives.

Two months later, we invite our client to a power breakfast (people are at their best early in the day). During the breakfast we work lightly on strengthening our relationship with the client, and then we discuss the evaluation results. We talk about what the results mean for improved employee performance and expectations and about the future needs of the company. In order to make solid recommendations, your AAR must include all of these parts. We find that our clients suggest a follow-up session 93 percent of the time.

Additionally, clients often mention other departments or colleagues that may be in need of our services. We're always casual in our approach; we listen to the client; and we use lead-in questions that keep the conversation nonthreatening. Our company has made it a policy to use this strategy with all of our clients. Our clients see us as part of their team, and this type of strategy session brings creditability. We do less selling and more consulting.

If you're truly customer-focused, then this after-action review strategy will help your clients succeed. When clients succeed, so do you!

Lorinzo Foxworth, Sales Professional

Persistence pays

I am always reading stories about being persistent, and I have found that persistence definitely works.

I had been calling on a company for two years. Every three weeks I would phone or e-mail this potential client, and I sent a lot of notes with my business card. The first conversation I had with the contact was cold, but over time she became friendlier. Then one day, I got a call from her. She said, "I am going to make your day" and proceeded to give me two orders.

When I met the contact for the first time and sat down in her office, she pulled out a stack of my company letterheads and every business card I had ever sent her. There must have been 50 cards and notes in that drawer. She said, "See—persistence does pay off in the end," and she was right. It took me two years, but in the end I got the business and held onto it.

Tony Harrill, Sales Professional

Too poor to buy cheap

When I'm in a sales situation where I expect a low and very competitive initial price to be a big issue, I like to open up with this question:

"How many of you in the room consider yourself rich?"

No one has ever raised a hand. I continue, "I am not rich, either. In fact, I once paid $100 for a suit!" The audience then looks confused. "That's right, and I wore it only once. I didn't like the way it looked on me, so I never wore it again! Boy, was that an expensive suit. If I had invested in a $300 suit the first time, I would have *saved* money by spending only $300 instead of $400.

"That's an example of why we all need to spend our money with the long-term cost in mind. Sometimes spending more money today saves even more money in the future."

Rob Koshkarian, Sales Professional

> **"The ability to simplify means to eliminate the unnecessary so that the necessary may speak."**
>
> **HANS HOFMANN**

Lessons for the teacher

My most memorable sale was made ... by the client himself! To him-

self! On my behalf! He was an executive with a manufacturing giant on

the West Coast. I was just starting my company and was thrilled to

have landed a contract with his company. The contract was for a train-

ing program dealing with effective communications, and he was one of

my students.

> **"Kindness effects more than severity."**
>
> AESOP

In the last of the 10 sessions, I went through the

usual closure. I summarized the main points. I told

the class members what they should do to engage in

continuous learning. I dealt with the evaluation

forms. I packed up. I said good-bye. I left.

As I approached the guard station to turn in my security badge, I

heard a voice behind me. The client stopped me with a question: "Why

are you leaving?" And then and there, he gave me a much-deserved lecture. "Why aren't you stopping by my desk to ask about future needs? To share your insights about our skill levels? To sell me more training programs? Your problem, Marlene, is that you have only excellence. But excellence is not enough. You need hype, and you have none. If you want to succeed in business," he advised me, "you need equal amounts of both!"

With that, he strode away. The guard had the kindness to avert his eyes and pretend he hadn't heard my comeuppance. I rushed back to the office, called the client, and asked about his future needs. I shared my insights about skill levels. I sold him another training program.

Marlene Caroselli, Sales Professional

Probing question blues

Learning to ask probing questions without feeling like I was being nosy or irritating was a stumbling block for me early on. A sales pro pointed out to me one day that a probing question merely shows real interest in your prospect's business needs.

He asked me a few probing questions: "When you talk to your friends and family, what kinds of things do you ask them? Don't you ask what they liked about the movie or the dinner? Do you ask them what they did over the weekend? How about what they saw or did on vacation? All of these are probing questions, but you didn't feel like you were being nosy, did you? Weren't you really showing that you were truly interested in them?"

When he put it that way, I began to see that conversational give-and-take is critical to sales success. I made it a point to pay attention to the way I talked with family members, friends, and coworkers. The old pro was exactly on target! And I gained a whole new level of comfort with the discovery process.

Linda Meehan, Sales Professional

Be a resource

Keeping your name in front of the customer or prospect is key. You don't always have to be face-to-face with your customers to strengthen your relationship and let them know you are trying to help their business grow.

One way of doing this is to mail or e-mail articles that pertain to your product or solution. These articles could be about your product specifically or about your industry in general and the cost savings or revenue growth other businesses are realizing by using what you provide.

> **"I hate the giving of the hand unless the whole man accompanies it."**
>
> **RALPH WALDO EMERSON**

Doing this will help you stay in front of your customer, especially important with new prospects or with customers you have not spoken with in a while. It's also a good opener for current customers you are trying to upsell or cross-sell. Furthermore, if the customer is considering your solution among others, this strategy will help build credibility and additional interest in your particular offering.

Read trade magazines that pertain to your industry, and look at Web sites for articles that your customers would like to read. Your customer may be very busy, so try to find articles that are fairly short.

Aaron Krause, Sales Professional

Reverse psychology

My most memorable sale was last year. I sell new construction in new communities. I was working in New York, and a very nice couple kept returning and returning, but always had a reason they could not buy just then. Finally, on a busy Sunday they came in with still more questions—and the prices had increased dramatically. I answered them and nicely told them that, as much as I enjoyed their visits, I did not believe they would buy a new home, and I had to continue with other clients. Now I believe in reverse psychology, because they pulled out their checkbook and bought the $650,000 townhome. You never know!

Maura Cannon, Sales Professional

Countdown to referrals

Here's a surefire way to increase the number of referrals you get. After you make your presentation to your customer on how you grow your business through qualified referrals, pull out a sheet printed with blanks for the following information: name, address, city, state, zip code, and telephone (home and office).

> ### "Pleasing ware is half sold."
>
> **GEORGE HERBERT**
>
>

Have slots on your page for five referrals. With your pen in hand and in close view of your client, begin with number 5 and work your way up the page until you have filled in all five contacts.

Your customer, seeing you start down at number 5 as opposed to starting at the top with number 1, will be more inclined to give you the five referrals. In other words, starting at number 5 and working backward makes it more likely that all the slots will be filled in. By securing all five referrals, your chances of getting more sales increase dramatically.

Michael J. Hoffman, Sales Professional

Analyze your performance

You ask your customers questions all day long to discover their needs—why not turn the tables and start asking yourself some questions after sales calls? With some honest soul-searching, you might discover a few things about yourself. Try the following questions:

- How did I appear to that customer? Was I confident and knowledgeable? Did I use powerful descriptions to differentiate the benefits of my product?

- Did I determine the customer's needs? Was there anything else I could have offered to explain or demonstrate?

- What objections to the product did the customer have? Did I respond with reasons why the product would actually benefit the customer by saving money or time? Did I sell peace of mind? Did I sell convenience? Did I sell prestige? Did I, in fact, start building a lifetime relationship with that customer?

- What were my preconceived expectations? Did I plan to make a sale, or was I prepared for the customer to walk away? Did I present all the facts and offer alternatives?

This short but insightful analysis practiced daily can help you become a more tuned-in and successful sales professional.

Linda Meehan, Sales Professional

Expect the unexpected

As the sales and marketing director for a large commercial cleaning services firm, I am always looking for ways to keep my name in front of my potential clients. I have found great success with a direct mail program that I developed for my top 100 prospects.

At the beginning of each year I come up with a plan for bimonthly mailers to send to my prospects. Most salespeople for cleaning companies just make a phone call to their prospects every month, and I found that buyers are put off by this lazy attempt to stay in touch.

Each of our mailers includes a small promotional item, but I always add a twist to it. For instance, one month I mailed out a computer duster that looked like a cow, but I mailed it in a milk carton with my photo on it (with a caption that said "Have you seen this woman"). The carton also had a side that read, "Got Dirt?" Another side gave nutritional information that read, "Serving Size: 1 building."

Another month I mailed out toy limousines along with a card that gave recipients a chance to win a night on the town with free limousine service and a gift certificate for dinner at a favorite restaurant. They had to e-mail or call me to enter the contest, and I had a 10 percent response. Each month, people call me to comment on the mailers, often mentioning how much everyone in the office enjoyed them. I always include a small, printed, postcard-size piece with the mailer that mentions the new accounts we just landed or some of our larger existing accounts, keeping the advertising message short so people will read it.

The bottom line is that people like something unexpected. I don't spend a lot on the mailers, and they are not done by an advertising agency. People appreciate something that is creative and off the wall. And they remember the rep who sent it!

Jane DiRoss, Sales and Marketing Director

Multiple choice

When I hear, "I want to think it over," instead of drilling my prospects I put them at ease by saying, "You know, Ms. Prospect, when someone tells me they want to think about a decision, it usually means (1) they feel the price is too high or value is too low, (2) they don't believe in my company, my product, or me, (3) they're afraid of making a mistake, (4) they sense the product may be more troublesome than the problem, (5) they think the product will soon be obsolete, or (6) there's some other reason for not making a decision. Would you share which category you fall into?" This approach usually convinces my prospects to open up so I can help them without interrogating them.

Carlos Llarena, Sales Professional

> **"Nothing is more difficult, and therefore more precious, than to be able to decide."**
>
> **NAPOLEON**

Getting the word out

I'm vice president of sales for a small company that uses outside man-ufacturer representatives to sell its products. Most of these agencies have various product lines. We all compete for their time. I found that a useful way to get out product information, promotional updates, and so forth was what I call my "Friday e-mail."

Every Thursday night I put out a one-page e-mail to each of the 100 reps who sell our products. On Friday morning when they turn on their computers my e-mail gives them up-to-date product information, promo-tion reminders, weekly specials, success stories, and any other useful information they can use for the following week.

The feedback I have received from the salespeople is that this simple one-page e-mail is the best and most-read communication they get. It's precise, simple, and takes only seconds to read.

Larry Easterlin, Vice President

Referrals— a gold mine

Every salesperson recognizes the power of referrals. The problem is remembering to ask for them.

Some salespeople hesitate to ask for referrals if the prospect doesn't buy. This is the wrong thing to do, because if a good presentation was made, prospects may feel obligated, since they didn't buy, to help the salesperson.

Here is the secret: After asking for a referral, inquire, "What do you admire most about the person you are referring?" Then, when you meet with referrals, start off by telling them about the good traits their friend admires them for. They will listen forever.

This is one of the most important lessons I've ever learned in my 65 years of selling.

Stanley E. Whitlatch, Sales Professional

Drive-by sales

In our territory, we do what we call a *drive-by* while we are out making sales calls. A drive-by is an unscheduled visit to a prospect, a client, or a company that you do not know anything about.

These visits help keep you fresh in the minds of clients, plus they help you discover new prospects in the area that you may not otherwise have been aware of. Whatever you call a drive-by in your territory, it is something that all successful sales reps do. However, when I have been on the road for a while and all I can think about is my next appointment or getting back to the office, motivating myself to make an extra stop can be quite a challenge. To keep myself going, I recall the advice my father would share with me on our road trips. These words of wisdom would come right after a big bug splattered across the windshield: "Any old bug can hit the windshield, but it takes one with guts to stick to it."

Always keep going. Your next big sale could be from that one extra drive-by.

JoAnn Rash, Sales Professional

Three's the charm

Sales reps on the road have three very important ways to keep their clients informed: visiting, calling, and mailing. (E-mail is a popular communication, but is not as effective, as it is too easily disposable.)

Visits, phone calls, and mailings are all excellent ways to communicate, and they work especially well in a combination of all three, which will guarantee successful sales. Your visits put a face with your voice, and in most cases your customer can see the products. Your phone calls take less of the customer's time, but they keep both of you informed and in touch. Mailings let you show your creative side and can deliver a huge amount of information.

The combination of these three forms of communication will put you at the top of your game and will boost your selling power.

Denise Cavanaugh, Sales Professional

"Even when I was young I suspected that much might be done in a better way."

HENRY FORD, SR.

Create a partnership

Salespeople who go into a call without a partnering mentality are missing the boat. To help you keep the customer in mind at all times, use the word *we* and get rid of the word *I*.

I learned this lesson the hard way.

On a call a few years ago, I kept on repeating the word *I*. "I can give you this." "I can help you with that." "I know what you need." "I've seen this before."

Finally the prospect turned to me and said: "It sounds as if you're selling this service to yourself. Are you that unsure of its value?"

It only took me a second to realize that he was right. So I asked if *we* could start again, and I've been using that strategy ever since. I consider all my prospects and customers my partners. We're in it together, and that concept has helped me build a successful territory.

Julia Louis, Major Accounts Executive

Avoid "code red"

When a client asks, "When can you have it ready?" we sellers immediately go into "code red" to come up with the earliest, and usually unreasonable, time we can deliver the product. But why go there?

> **"It is the man determines what is said, not the words."**
>
> HENRY DAVID THOREAU

Instead, if you simply ask the client, "Is time a problem for you?" you will know the real time frame that will make the client happy. In most cases, the client will respond with a much more reasonable time of delivery than you have imposed on yourself. On the other hand, if the client does expect an unreasonable delivery date, you can decide whether you want to break your neck to get it done.

Keep in mind that whenever you take on an unreasonable delivery date, someone in production and shipping will often have to drop what they are doing, which may create a delivery problem somewhere else. Also realize that when you promise a lightning-fast delivery date, if you're one minute late (even if it's in world-record speed) you have failed in the customer's eyes.

Wallie B. Jones, Sales Professional

The backbone of sales

I am a senior account executive with a large publicly traded telemarketing company based in New Jersey. I sell practice-building telecommunication services to doctors of chiropractic nationwide.

I landed the biggest and most memorable sale of my career through a cold call. I had read a powerful article in a chiropractic magazine. I was so impressed with the doctor in this article and his drive for success that I had to share with him how my services might be able to help him reach even greater success. It took three letters and an endless number of messages, personal notes, articles, and anything else I could get my hands on to prove to him that I had his best interests in mind. Six months later I landed the sale, which over the past four years has led to more than $375,000 in business for my company and a large referral-based database for me.

Cold calling works. Persistence works. Dedication and commitment work.

Ronnie Gallucci, Senior Account Executive

Get past the gatekeeper

Salespeople are often frustrated when they can't get past a protective secretary to talk to the qualified buyer. Consequently, they will give a presentation to a nonqualified buyer as a last resort. "He will call you if he is interested" is the usual remark. Trouble is, a secretary will not present a salesperson's product or service in a professional way. We wish it were that simple. Here are a few techniques to help you get past gatekeepers:

1. Call when you think they might be at lunch and your prospect has to answer the phone.

2. Ask for help. "I need help," or "I wonder if you could help me." Another question is, "Could you tell me when it would be a good time to call?"

3. Make the gatekeeper feel important.

4. Build rapport. Ask the secretary's name (write it down), and then use it when you call again. You may use, "Hope you had a good weekend, Pat."

5. Respect the gatekeeper's position.

6. A sense of humor helps, but be careful. Be subtle. If you aren't naturally humorous, don't push it.

7. Never, ever alienate gatekeepers. The higher the level, the more power they have.

8. Be nice to everyone you speak to. That person may get promoted.

9. Always use Mr. or Ms. unless told otherwise. (Honey or sweetheart is a death sentence.)

10. To qualify a gatekeeper you can ask, "Are you _____'s assistant?"

11. When receiving resistance, such as, "He is on the phone" or "She is in a meeting," make a second try. Don't offend the secretary by refusing to answer the question "Is there something I can help you with?"

12. Use a hinge—a personal referral, a letter you sent, or a meeting you had with the prospect.

Be persistent, but not obnoxious. If it is urgent, say so; if not, don't say so. The gatekeeper is important. Don't mess it up.

Carl E. Blinnel, Sales Trainer

Agree with objections

Every product or service sold has at least one flaw, and overcoming the objections that arise from these shortcomings is what often separates a good salesperson from a great salesperson.

In real estate sales, all homes have flaws—and customers generally find those flaws. Whether it is a room that is too small or a community that borders on a main road, I have found that it can be a good approach to flat out agree with the objection if it is valid. The bottom line is that, if the room is small, all of my talking won't make it any larger. I may choose to focus instead on whether the whole house has enough going for it to meet my customer's overall needs.

We tend to get caught up in proving our cause so much that we overlook the importance of validating legitimate concerns. Furthermore, customers look to disqualify a salesperson on the basis of trust early in the process, even on what we may consider small issues. Brutal honesty is a form of empathy. It shows character and ultimately builds credibility and trust. You would be surprised how many customers have bought homes from me with small rooms and next to main roads.

Andy Goodman, Sales Professional

Discover the pain

To help prospects self-discover their pain, ask probing questions that secure psychological permission from them to probe deeper for the root problem. While the questions you ask are probing in nature, each will also establish the psychological permission you need to ask another question until you reach a prospect's emotional bedrock, the real issue or problem that needs solving. The self-discovery questioning sequence is: Probe, permission, problem.

When the opportunity presents itself, probe deeper with these questions: Tell me more about that. Could you be more specific about . . . ? How long has this been a problem? How have you tried to solve this problem? Has the solution worked to your satisfaction? How does that make you feel?

When you hit sales pay dirt, the prospect's emotional bedrock, your solution has the greatest value.

John O'Malley, Sales Professional

Have a contingency plan

When making a presentation, you always need a contingency plan.

My most memorable sale took about two years. When you are dealing with a decision to spend millions of dollars, sometimes that decision takes a while. Driving the sale, I directed the buyers to narrow their interest to three companies offering similar solutions in the usual show-and-tell presentation format. The competition was fierce, and we made the first presentation.

Lots of people will tell you that going first is not the best position to be in, but we wanted to set the bar high and have the decision makers in the freshest frame of mind, so we asked to go first. That decision proved to be the right one.

The presentation consisted of prepared slides that would be displayed to a group of 15 decision makers. We prepared our presentation in the usual format and began fine-tuning our presentation through role-playing. One of my team members suggested that we also prepare color transparencies in the event of a computer meltdown. I laughed at that idea and even recall saying something like "My computer has never frozen, so I don't think that's necessary." Believe it or not, my team agreed with me because I was the quarterback.

The night prior to the "big day," I could not sleep because of the haunting nightmare of my computer crashing. I finally got out of bed around 3 a.m. and drove to my office to begin the arduous task of backing up the presentation with color transparencies for an old-fashioned overhead projector. Wrapping up the task, I grabbed that dusty projector and the transparency folder and off we went at 7 a.m. for the biggest presentation of my career.

Arriving early, we prepared the screen, LCD projector, and laptop. I plugged in the overhead projector and made sure it was ready to go. Little did I know that the old dusty overhead projector and transparencies were not prepared in vain.

After the fifth slide, my laptop froze. Without missing a beat, my teammates immediately placed the overhead projector on top of my laptop computer and went to the very next slide. I worked the mistake into the presentation by telling the group that you always need a contingency plan, especially when renovating facilities.

I found out afterward, when we were selected as the "contractor of choice," that our backup plan so impressed many of the decision makers that it was one of the key factors in the decision they made to contract with us.

William Krol, Manager, Sales Development

A little extra punch

Many salespeople use traditional invitations or announcements to focus attention on seminars, offer new products, or sometimes just acquaint a prospect with their name and company. These types of mailings typically include a printed or handwritten message as well as a business card held in place with die-cut slits. For certain businesses, mailings like this can be productive, but they can be exponentially more productive with a little extra effort.

We all think we are good copywriters, and perhaps the message on your mailing is truly great, but here's how to deliver a little extra punch.

> **"Man's rise or fall, success or failure, happiness or unhappiness depends on his attitude . . . a man's attitude will create the situation he imagines."**
>
> **JAMES LANE ALLEN**

Imagine a prospect opening and reading your message. He or she could be interested and keep it, or disinterested and chuck it. But either way, most prospects will remove your business card. That's where you deliver the extra punch. Behind where the card sits is a perfect place to surprise them with an incentive. It could be an extra percentage off, seating in the front row, a buffet in your hospitality suite, or a two-for-one offer, but whatever it is, it's one additional shot to increase interest and the likelihood that your message will make a lasting impression. You can increase the chances that they will remove your card by letting the hidden message "hang out" slightly from behind the card.

Steve Donovan, Sales Professional

Confidence gained

I was a new salesperson struggling to find my identity, and I felt that I lacked the confidence and assertiveness to become a successful salesperson. But when a call came in from a West Coast customer seeking a price and delivery quotation on a part, I jumped in to provide prompt and satisfactory customer service. I took the order and shipped out the product and immediately called the customer back with the tracking number. I then asked if there was anything else I could help him out with.

This customer politely declined, saying that he appreciated my help but was happy with his current local West Coast vendor. Simple research uncovered the facts that the person I was talking to represented a $300,000 account, and his needs were a good match for our products and services.

This same customer called a handful of times over the next six months, and each time I asked if he would allow me the opportunity to quote on his entire package of parts. Each time he thanked me, and politely declined saying that he was happy with his current supplier.

I was careful not to bad-mouth his supplier, but it was apparent to me (and to him) that his supplier was not doing a good job. Finally the customer relented and allowed me to quote on his package, and I landed the account!

From this point, my confidence grew. Good customer service, patience, and persistence had finally paid off.

Brian M. Wahl, Sales Professional

The daily commitment

One way to stay focused is to have daily goals.

As a sales manager, one of the most important responsibilities I have is to train my staff. I am always looking for ways to improve my training techniques, theories, and practices. However, I have learned over the years that you can overtrain to the point that the focus will be lost.

I try to keep my staff members focused on the basics of selling and then let their imaginations work from there. We have what we call the "Daily Commitment."

1. *See enough people.* We require all of our salespeople to have six prescheduled appointments before they leave the office.

2. *Sell something.* We realize that it is not always possible to sell something every day. However, we must keep them focused on attempting to sell something every day.

3. *Do today's paperwork today.* Do not carry over your paperwork into tomorrow. The delay is a big time waster, and there will be a greater chance for errors.

4. *Do your scheduled follow-ups.* You cannot allow yourself to follow up on only certain days of the week. Your competition will be following up every day.

5. *Set up enough appointments today for a full, productive tomorrow.* If you don't plan your day in advance, it will plan itself for you, and you will not be as productive.

Larry Akin, Sales Manager

Break down to win

To set goals you can meet, break down your huge aspirations into smaller ones. For instance, instead of saying, "I want to be thin," break down how much weight it would be necessary to lose to be considered thin, and then break down that weight into daily increments.

Breaking down goals truly is critical. For example, let's assume you want to earn $100,000 this year in production. If the goal is too big, it doesn't seem attainable, but if I asked you to try to earn $208, how does that sound?

Here's what I do. On a piece of paper I draw three columns: Date, Forecast, and Actual. The amount of $100,000 can be broken into monthly production. Monthly can be broken into daily (20 business days). Daily can be broken into what you need by lunch and what is needed by the time you go home, or else don't go home.

Therefore, $100,000 becomes $8,333 a month, or $416 a day, or $208 by lunch and $208 before you go home. You see how easy it is to earn $100,000?

In the columns, here is what to do, assuming the goal of $100,000.

Date: Today. Forecast: $416. Actual: Write the number you actually earned for the day. Let's assume you had a bad day and didn't earn anything. The $416 is added back into the remaining days of the month. Thus, if it is the first day, divide $416 by the remaining 19 days, and tomorrow's forecast would be $438. All the remaining days' forecast will never be less than $438, even if you earn $1,000 in one day; the additional money you earn just becomes gravy. So, on the second day if your forecast is $438 and you earned $500, the third day forecast remains $438.

I believe any success I've had in sales has been due in large part to setting goals, writing them down, and becoming obsessed about following them. I keep a copy on my desk in the office, a copy at home, and a minimized copy in my wallet. It is always in my face. At the end of the month when I reach my goal, and only when I reach it, I reward myself with a gift.

This will separate you from the mediocrity out there.

Gregory Manto, Sales Professional

Keep your cool

Showing my prospect that I could handle pressure showed I could also handle his business.

When I first moved to Chicago to run the Midwest sales office for APAC TeleServices, I went after some big accounts and eventually got a callback from a very large retailer who requested a proposal. Four months after I presented a proposal for almost $1 million in services, the prospect called and invited me to lunch. As dessert was being served, my client told me he didn't know whether to entrust me with his business or give it to a similarly priced and qualified competitor. He told me he was going to flip a coin to decide, and that if I called the toss correctly, I could have the business.

> **"From a man's face, I can read his character . . ."**
>
> **PETRONIUS**

I felt the color drain from my face. My palms began to sweat as I realized my client was serious, but I tried to maintain a composed facade and called "heads" as he tossed the coin. Heads it was, fortunately, and

I got the order. After some time, I asked my client why he had decided to base such an important decision on a coin toss. He confessed that he had already decided to work with my company before he flipped the coin, but that because I had seemed so calm and cool up until then he wanted to see if he could make me squirm. When I didn't, he said that proved to him that I wouldn't fall apart when a big challenge presented itself. Showing my prospect that I could handle pressure showed I could also handle his business.

Hayley Weinper, Sales Professional

Beat the competition

Beat the competition. This axiom went along with the sign over my desk, which admonishes, "If nobody ever sells, nobody eats." Competition was very much on my mind as I set out to respond to a call from a subsidiary of one of my major competitors. My task: To provide an enhanced operating system for my competitor's mainframe computers.

Armed with a slide presentation and sufficient literature for 50 percent more than the anticipated 10 people, I planned a standard hour-and-a-half presentation of my very complex subject. The interest level was high, mainly because the home office of my potential customer—which was supplying its operating system—was not responding to their problems or to their requests for improvements. They needed help.

As each person came into the room, I introduced myself, noted their name and function, and asked them frankly what difficulties they were experiencing and what they thought they needed. As the presentation began—to double the expected audience—I warmed to my subject and began pointing out specific benefits to specific members of the group to meet their specific difficulties and needs, all the while reinforcing my points with success stories and references. They began to be drawn in, and questions and explanations grew. The coffee wagon and lunch cart came by and left, and no one made a move because they didn't want to miss anything.

When we finally tied things up after four hours, I was exhilarated. I had made not just another sale over the competition, but a sale *to* the competition!

Sam Holland, Sales Professional

"What's the next step?"

The most important question you can ask your sales force when reviewing potential opportunities is "What's the next step?" Ask this enough and it will become so ingrained that they will ask themselves the question before you do. Too many times, salespeople leave an appointment feeling good about the probability of a closed sale only to answer the preceding question with, "They said I'd hear from them next week," or "I'm supposed to call them in two weeks for a decision."

Countless articles and books are written about effective cold calling, all geared to getting an appointment in order to start the sales cycle. Why, then, would a salesperson get battered and bloody making these appointments, only to leave them without a concrete next step? What is a concrete next step? Another appointment!

Breaking contact with a prospect without setting a next step length-ens the sales cycle because of the possible delays in reconnecting via voice mail and e-mail. It also slows the emotional momentum, which weakens the sense of urgency. To close sales more quickly, there must be emotion attached to the process—not just to the product. Without this, "They said I'd hear from them next week" actually turns into months, and the salesperson is left scratching his or her head.

The next-step strategy is also a good trial close and litmus test for how serious the prospect is. If the salesperson encounters resistance when trying to set that next appointment, it's a clear sign that there is an objection still left on the table—one that would have gone unno-ticed until the final decision has been made in the competition's favor.

The easiest way to encourage your sales force to use this strategy consistently is to incorporate it into your meeting agendas. "The next step" should be the final item on every agenda. One of the main goals of a sales appointment is to dig beyond the nebulous answers prospects

have been trained to respond with in order to feign interest or to avoid

uncomfortable conversations. This is one more tool you can use to figure

out whether an opportunity is viable or just someone "kicking the tires."

It also keeps that ball rolling downhill along a predefined path toward the

signature on the contract and money in the bank.

David McGeogh, Regional Manager

Recognition rocks reps

All salespeople respond to some form of recognition. Recognition can

take many forms—rewards like gifts or gift cards, praise in sales

meetings or in front of the top brass, awards in the

form of plaques or letters, cash bonuses, and many

other forms. The key for managers to remember is this:

Recognition should not be saved up like a bank account

and dipped into only on very special occasions. Recog-

nition in some form should be ongoing throughout the

> **"Foolish are the generals who ignore the daily information from the trenches."**
>
> **ANONYMOUS**

year. Praise is simple and inexpensive. It only takes a minute of your

time to give out a pat on the back or a "Job well done, Joe." Do it often.

Do it with feeling. Do it because it feels good.

Alan Cervasio, Vice President
Global Sales Strategy and Talent Management

A little at a time

Psychologists tell us that most people are much more apt to say yes to a new idea if it is presented to them a little at a time. But if the entire matter is thrust at them in one big piece, they probably will turn it down fast.

Publicists put this psychological quirk to practical use; so do teachers. Physicians apply it in healing mental diseases. It has dollars-and-cents value in selling, and many of us use it, perhaps without giving it conscious thought. Its importance was brought home to me again recently when my little nephew, Buster, came to visit me over the holidays.

My nephew wanted a dollar when we first met—he would put it in his bank. The idea was good. Built up by his approach, I bought. Later he asked me for a dollar for another good reason—ice cream. And so on!

He stayed for four days, and after he left, I recovered from exhaustion and realized he had obtained $10 from me. If he had asked me for $10 when we first met, I would have hung him from the nearest lamp-post. But he did it step by step, every time presenting a need that was appealing and logical. What could anyone do but fill each one as it came along?

Buster collected $10 from me, but he reminded me of the importance of that bit of practical psychology in selling. The successful salesperson uncovers the prospect's needs and pictures them in such a personal, appealing way that the prospect can't help but want to fill them. But if the salesperson senses that the prospect can't or won't fill them all at one time, he or she concentrates on the paramount one, taking care of the others gradually and in due time.

> **"Give every man thine ear, but few thy voice."**
>
> **SHAKESPEARE**

To ask for the whole $10 at once is to gamble on all or nothing—with the odds usually on nothing. To ask for it a little at a time, with each appeal touching the prospect's basic emotions, is to be almost certain of the getting the whole thing.

Caesar P. Tabet, Sales Professional

Create objections and close

One way to prevent a prospect's objections is by creating your own. If you introduce ridiculous terms of the sale—terms you can easily eliminate—you often can get the client to agree on a purchase.

Let's see how it works. Ridiculous terms can be anything from a crazy time schedule ("If I put in your application today, I can get it approved in three or four months") to outlandish demands ("It's company policy for me to get 20 referrals from each of our clients").

Naturally the client will object. Now you can say, "You mean I don't get your order unless I can have your application approved immediately?" or "Are you saying that I won't get your account unless I agree to accept only three names?" (or however many the client indignantly offers to provide).

In essence, such clients are saying that only if you agree to their (reasonable) terms will they buy. So go ahead, agree to be reasonable, and close. Rather than waiting for clients to come up with an objection you can't eliminate, instead hand them one that you can.

Bill Bishop, Author, Speaker, and
College Instructor of Salesmanship

A classified success

As the president of my own company, I have made it a habit to peruse the Sunday classified section for organizations that might need my company's services. One Sunday I saw an ad looking for a "conference planner" for a scientific symposium being developed by the University of California, Davis. The ad also requested a commitment of one year. Even though they were looking for an individual, I filled out the online application and forwarded my company's information in hopes they would consider contracting with me.

As it ended up, I received a call from the university planners inviting me to meet with them. At that time, I was able to go into detail about how my company could help satisfy their needs.

They agreed and hired my company to plan their symposium for the next year. In addition, after I was hired, I found out that the university

has a partnership to help plan this symposium, as well other projects
throughout the year, with a $14 billion global corporation. Because of
our solid work, discussions have now begun on how to continue our relationship after the symposium concludes.

I firmly believe that the classifieds are a great way of prospecting.

Jennifer D. Collins, President

Little things add up

My first sales job was in the summer of 1985, selling computers in a small retail store filled with experienced salespeople. I was told to stand at the front of the store and make my calls using the phone behind the sales counter. When a customer entered the store, all the other salespeople would scatter like mice, leaving me to take care of the customers' needs. It did not take long to see why they ran from these customers. In my first three months, I sold nothing more than printer ribbons and paper and barely made any commissions.

Then an interesting thing happened. As the Christmas holiday approached, everyone prepared to earn huge commissions. As expected, customers flocked into our store; however, something unexpected happened: The majority of the customers who came into the store asked for me. Because I had greeted just about every customer for the past six months, they all wanted to buy from the person who took the time to take care of them. As a result, I became Salesman of the Quarter, and my sales career was launched. Today, no matter how insignificant a lead might seem, I still always make it a priority to enthusiastically give every prospect a call.

Scott Mitchell, Sales Professional

Rotate your inventory

I learned a valuable selling idea from a used-car dealer when I commented on how fast he sold cars. He explained that every morning his first self-appointed task involved moving every car on the lot to a different location. He went on to say that besides making the lot seem busy, moving vehicles himself made him constantly see his product from the customers' perspective. When he slid behind the wheel and turned the key he felt, heard, smelled, and saw just what his prospects experienced, and whatever struck him as wrong was immediately fixed.

I thought about my own "car lot" and decided to apply his ideas to my selling. I put fresh samples in a calfskin binder, bought new clothes, gave my Web site a makeover, and ordered different business cards. I pulled out the video camera and filmed myself "selling" products. Viewing the tape, I was amazed how much my presentations needed to change!

That was several months ago. Since then, my sales have shown a comfortable increase, and I have decided to make changing my "car lot" an annual event.

Stephen K. Donovan, Sales Professional

Just say no

My most memorable sale started when I said no to a potentially huge client. I provide presentation-skills training to sales teams and managers. I got a call earlier this year from a prospective client who was new in town and found my speaking company through a training association.

The call went like this: "I'm calling from a division of Pfizer here in San Diego. We are hosting a group of 80 to 100 doctors for a conference next month. We are looking for a speaker to come in and talk for an hour about giving presentations. We'd like the talk to be fun and humorous, and it will be a good chance for you to promote your company and other resources the doctors might want to use in the future around the country."

> **"Trust men and they will be true to you . . ."**
>
> **RALPH WALDO EMERSON**

Initially I was very excited, but I asked the prospect if I could call him back in a little while. After considering the audience of doctors speaking to other doctors, my own experience in that field, which was none, and the fact that I did not have a national company, I had my doubts.

I called the prospect back and told him that I wasn't the best person to work with this audience. I asked if I could meet him and learn more about his training responsibilities.

It turned out that he was responsible for training the national sales force of pharmaceutical reps. Over the next six months, I worked with several of their sales teams around the country. I also delivered training for a group of physicians who were going to be educating other physicians about treating patients with HIV/AIDS. I had learned enough about the company by that time that I felt confident I could deliver a great training program to them, and I did.

By turning down a job that I did not feel qualified to handle at the time, I developed an instant trust with my contact. That trust led to business I did feel confident about handling.

Dana Bristol Smith, Sales Consultant

Quick returns

Don't make it more difficult—or even impossible—for prospects to reach you. Think of the times you listened to a long message that went on and on, and then you couldn't return the call because the caller said the phone number in one nanosecond. What did you do? Maybe you listened to the entire message again, just to hear the number. Or perhaps you saved the message for a later time. If it was really a bad day, maybe you just deleted the message.

To make it easy for your clients or prospects to return your calls, repeat your number twice—and say it no faster than you can write it down. Jazz up the ending to your message if you want. Just remember to make it easy for clients to call you and not your competitors.

Patrick Shemek, Account Executive

"This is a cold call . . ."

To break through the clutter of calls your prospects receive, try being honest from the beginning by saying, "This is a cold call . . . want to hang up now?" Most people will laugh or say, "That's a new one." Then they will ask you what you are selling. It's magical. You made a cold call, and in 10 seconds they are asking you what you sell. The only danger with this one-liner is that you have to use the right tone. If you sound bored or frustrated, prospects will want to hang up. Have some fun with this one, and they will, too.

Merit Gest, Sales Professional

Create your own unforgettable introduction

Years ago, during less-sensitive times, I had a difficult time getting the CEO of a national nonprofit to return my phone calls. Although I had a wonderful relationship with his voice mail, I was never able to speak to him, regardless of what time I called.

Someone mentioned in passing about struggling to get her foot in the door of a company she was trying to sell to, and an idea hit me! The next day, I went to the local shopping mall and purchased a pair of dress shoes. I wrapped one up and sent it by courier to the CEO. Upon opening the package, he read the note on my business card: "John, now that I finally have one foot in the door, may I bring the other in to join it?"

His administrative assistant called me first thing the following morning to schedule a time to meet.

John liked my persistence, but he loved my creativity. He told me he could comfortably expect that same creativity to be dedicated to him from then on. Until I left that particular field of business, he remained one of my best clients. I even invited him to my wedding.

Sometimes being direct is the best way to get your foot in the door.

Stuart B. Margel, Sales Professional

Making the connection

I sell specialty metal products to commercial construction contractors in a large metropolitan territory. Here's the way I prospect for new business.

After checking recent construction permits that have been requested with the city, every Monday I spend the entire morning driving to the sites that match the permit applications and looking for any construction vehicles with the name of the contracting company that requested the permit.

Next I ask for the general contractor, introduce myself, and give him or her my card. Then I say I'll follow up with a phone call. Then I look for a good restaurant in the neighborhood and, when I call, I invite the contractor to lunch. If the contractor is too busy to take time out for lunch, I offer to bring it to the site. That usually goes over well, and it gives me a chance to ask about the job and the needs of the contractor.

After making this connection, it's usually easy to talk about what our company offers and ask if we can be of service. Then it's a matter of bidding and asking for the business.

I won't say it always gets me the business, but I would say it works about 50 percent of the time. Which is a pretty good success rate.

Haviland Plummer, Contractor Accounts Specialist

Go to meetin'

Acquire new sales ideas from colleagues in other industries by attending one of their sales or staff meetings. Many of us attend sales training where we interact with people from our own company or our own industry. Try something different: Ask customers or prospects you know well if you may attend one of their future sales/staff meetings, just as an observer.

You'd be surprised how important it makes your customers feel when you want to take the time to be present at their meetings. In most cases, they will introduce you to the group and allow you to speak a few minutes. Use this time to announce a new promotion or do a 60-second advertisement. It's a great way to promote a message to a group of people, solidify a current relationship, or establish a new one.

Second, you are afforded the opportunity to acquire new sales ideas, tactics, and alternative methods for conducting your own sales meetings.

Take some treats, so you may interact with the attendees before and after the meeting.

Andrew S. Kyres, Vice President, Business Development

Index of tip contributors

Akin, Larry, 229
Alcantar, Phillip D., 97
Alie, Stan, 30
Allen, Daryl A., 51
Alofs, John, 61
Amantea, Cheryl, 31
Ambrose, Tony, 177
Anderson, Cara, 21
Anderson, Carrie, 13
Aram, Brooke, 143
Atchison, Debbie, 20
Azevedo, Melissa, 163

Banks, Keith, 191
Batchelor, Angela, 37
Batdorff, Donna, 38
Beasley, Debra, 82
Bernius, Roy, 45
Bishop, Bill, 243
Blair, Grant, 181
Blinnel, Carl E., 217
Blumenschine,
   Leonard G., III, 76
Blunt, Dona, 52
Brezovski, Tony, 134
Bruno, Amy, 11
Burr, Jeff, 135

Cain, Cathy, 66
Cannon, Maura, 202
Capozzi, Vincent, 103
Caroselli, Marlene, 197
Catal, Joe, 141
Cavanaugh, Denise,
   212

Cervasio, Alan, 139,
   239
Cicatko, Anthony S.,
   Sr., 145
Cole, Ginger, 57
Colligan, Nancy, 100
Collins, Jennifer, 245
Collins, Patrick, 144
Colvin, Jeff, 33
Confrey, John R.
   (Jack), 161
Connor, Jane, 8
Cordes, Randy, 28
Corona, Lisa, 119
Craig, Rick, 72
Cullen, Bill, 96

Daniels, Marc, 179
DiRoss, Jane, 207
Donovan, Stephen K.
   (Steve), 87, 225, 249
Durall, Renita, 36

Easterlin, Larry, 25,
   209
Eaves, Roz, 44
Edelman, Lester, 10
Ehmann, Lain
   Chroust, 112
Engels, Donald J., Jr.,
   109
Esch, Traci, 80

Fahner, Mike, 169
Fedors, Paul, 115

Fitzpatrick, Ricky, 165
Ford, Robert, 56
Fossland, Joeann, 73
Foxworth, Lorinzo, 193
Freitag, Joan, 158, 164,
   180
Fullmer, Joel, 59

Gacke, Kristi, 113
Gallucci, Ronnie, 215
Galyean, Woody, 19
Garcia, Laura, 140
Gest, Merit, 253
Gilot, Bob, 185
Giudici, Carey, 108
Goldman, Marvin S., 41
Goldstein, Alan H., 90
Goodman, Andy, 219
Goodman, Dr. Gary, 98
Goodman, Harold, 173
Gordon, Carol, 55
Grady, Terry, 29
Greenhut, Kimberly,
   167
Gupta, Anup, 43

Hahn, Nancy, 24
Halo, George, 150
Harrill, Tony, 194
Hefner, Allen, 49
Hendon, Nelda, 17
Hill, Bob, 120
Hiskey, Peter, 175
Hoffman, Michael J.,
   203

Hogue, Mary Anne, 105
Holguin, Eder, 183
Holland, Sam, 235
Hooper, Dane, 91
Hoover, Gordon, 89
Horn, Justin A., 93
Huet, Micky, 131

Jackson, Christopher
O., 35
Jankowski, Jennifer,
92
Job, Terri, 23
Jones, Laurie, 22
Jones, Wallie, B., 214

Karycinski, Frank, 116
Katz, Barry, 39
Kelley, Debbie, 114
Kennedy, Philip, 148
Kester, Linda P., 104
Kirchner, John F., 127
Knutson, John, 47
Koivuniemi, Kari, 132
Koshkarian, Rob, 195
Krause, Aaron, 201
Kristoff, John, 75
Krol, William, 223
Kyres, Andrew S., 258

Lathrop, Brad R., 46
Linda Meehan, 205
Llarena, Carlos, 107,
208
Louis, Julia, 213
Lovat, Denise, 95

Malin, Lawrence A., 65
Manto, Gregory, 231
Margel, Stuart B., 255
Martin, Diana M., 94
Mashini, Diana, 26
McBride, Mark, 68
McCain, Steve, 130

McGeogh, David, 238
Meehan, Linda, 199,
205
Merwin, Tina, 123
Miller, Anne, 106
Mitchell, Scott, 247
Moorehead, Jim, 147
Moses, Christine, 83
Mosvick, James, 69

Nahrstedt, Don, 14
Naser, Shelley, 126
New, Ron, 155
Newbry, Donna M., 159
Nierenberg, Andrea, 15

Obermeyer, Michael
R., 149
O'Malley, John, 220

Parker, Sharon V., 152
Passaro, Rick, 78
Pehrson, Ralph, 9
Pels, Jule, 27
Peltz, Claude, 101
Pennington, Don, 110
Peters, Rita, 18
Peterson, Robert M.,
12
Pitney, Scott, 122
Pittendrigh, Steve, 81
Plummer, Haviland,
257
Pollak, Patricia, 128
Porter, Thomas B., 62
Potts, Lynn, 67
Poulin, Bruce, 182
Preston, Debbie, 125

Quatrini, John A., 40
Quintero, Kristen, 118

Raisin, John T., 42
Rash, JoAnn, 211

Reindl, Scott, 153
Reis, Mike, 129
Richardson, Anne, 60
Richardson, Darron,
34
Rowe, Dawn, 48

Sauerman, Gretchen,
79
Schrader, Lisa, 133
Schram, John, 70
Seib, John, 86
Shames, Debbie, 88
Shemek, Patrick, 162,
171, 252
Smith, Dana Bristol,
251
Sommella, Terri, 117
Steiner, Cathy, 137
Supplesa, John, 77
Swark, Kevin, 102

Tabet, Caesar P., 241
Taylor, Lynne M., 99
Tiso, Steven C., 187
Trinko, Tom, 63
Triplett, Jennifer, 71

Ubaldini, Michael, 151

Vogel, Erika, 136
Vosler, Angela, 121

Wahl, Brian, 227
Wallis, Wendy, 124
Warrington, Traci, 111
Warshofsky, Kelly, 189
Webb, Steve, 54
Weber, Mark, 157
Weinper, Hayley, 233
West, Robert N., 85
Whitlatch, Stanley E.,
210
Wilson, Thomas J., 53

About the Author

A dual citizen of both Austria and the United States, Gerhard Gschwandtner is the founder and publisher of *Selling Power,* the leading magazine for sales professionals worldwide, with a circulation of 165,000 subscribers in 67 countries.

He began his career in his native Austria in the sales training and marketing departments of a large construction equipment company. In 1972, he moved to the United States to become the company's North American Sales Training Director, later moving into the position of Marketing Manager.

In 1977, he became an independent sales training consultant, and in 1979 created an audiovisual sales training course called "The Languages of Selling." Marketed to sales managers at Fortune 500 companies, the course taught nonverbal communication in sales together with professional selling skills.

In 1981, Gerhard launched *Personal Selling Power,* a tabloid-format newsletter directed to sales managers. Over the years the tabloid grew in subscriptions, size, and frequency. The name changed to *Selling Power,* and in magazine format it became the leader in the professional sales field. Every year *Selling Power* publishes the "Selling Power 500," a listing of the largest sales forces in America. The company publishes books, sales training posters, and audio and video products for the professional sales market.

Gerhard has become America's leading expert on selling and sales management. He conducts webinars for such companies as SAP, and *Selling Power* has recently launched a new conference division that sponsors and conducts by-invitation-only leadership conferences directed toward companies with high sales volume and large sales forces.

For more information on *Selling Power* and its products and services, please visit www.sellingpower.com.

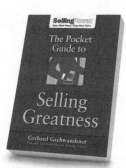

Subscribe to *Selling Power* today and close more sales tomorrow!

GET 10 ISSUES – INCLUDING *THE SALES MANAGER'S SOURCE BOOK.*

In every issue of *Selling Power* magazine you'll find:

■ **A Sales Manager's Training Guide** with a one-hour sales training workshop complete with exercises and step-by-step instructions. Get a new guide in every issue! Created by proven industry experts who get $10,000 or more for a keynote speech or a training session.

■ **Best-practices reports** that show you how to win in today's tough market. Valuable tips and techniques for opening more doors and closing more sales.

■ **How-to stories** that help you speed up your sales cycle with innovative technology solutions, so you'll stay on the leading edge and avoid the "bleeding edge."

■ **Tested motivation ideas** so you and your team can remain focused, stay enthusiastic and prevail in the face of adversity.

NEW! Digital Edition same as print. 100% online.

Plus, you can sign up for five online SellingPower.com newsletters absolutely FREE.

FOR FASTEST SERVICE CALL 800-752-7355
TO SUBSCRIBE ONLINE GO TO WWW.SELLINGPOWER.COM

I want a one-year subscription to *Selling Power* magazine.

☐ **YES!** Send me one year of the print edition for only $27
☐ **YES!** Sign me up for one year of the digital edition for only $19
☐ **YES!** Sign me up for one year of both for only $33

Please note: Subscriptions begin upon receipt of payment. For priority service include check or credit card information. Canadian and overseas subscriptions, please visit www.sellingpower.com for rates.

Name: _____ Title: _____

Company: _____

Address:_____

City: _____ State: _____ Zip: _____ Phone: _____

☐ Check enclosed   Charge my ☐ Visa ☐ MC ☐ AMEX ☐ Discover

Card number: _____ Exp.:_____

Name on card: _____ Signature: _____

For fastest service call 800-752-7355 • To subscribe online go to www.sellingpower.com